Practical
Palmistry

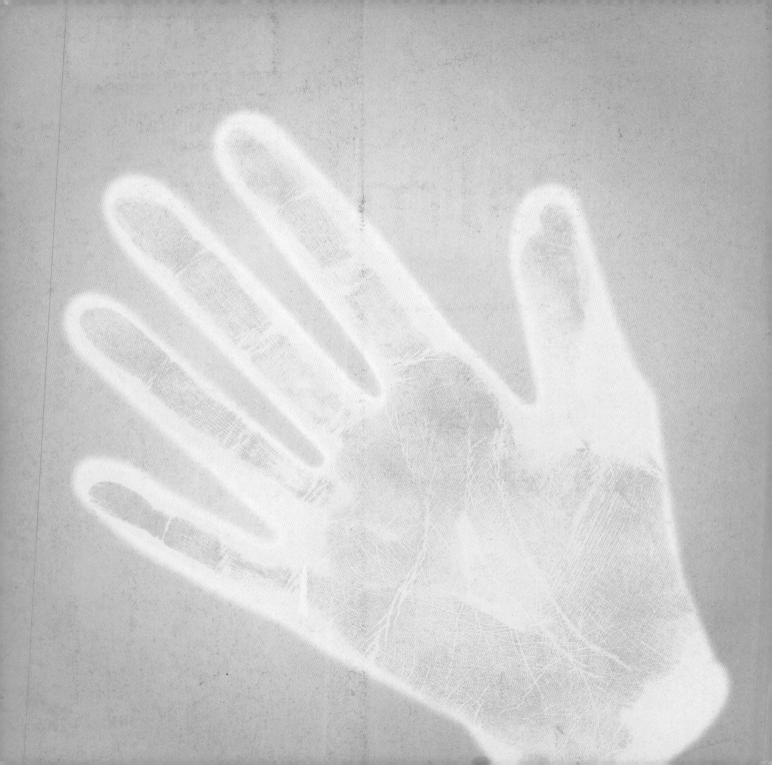

Practical Palmistry

COLLINS & BROWN

JON DATHEN

First published in Great Britain in 2003 by
Collins & Brown Limited
64 Brewery Road
London
N7 9NT

A member of **Chrysalis** Books plc

9 8 7 6 5 4 3 2 1

British Library Cataloguing-in-Publication Data: A catalogue record
for this book is available from the British Library

ISBN: 1-84340-029-4

Designed by Caroline Grimshaw
Edited by Lydia Derbyshire
Illustrations by Caroline Grimshaw and Monica Laita
Indexed by Margaret Binns
Project managed by Jane Ellis

Colour reproduction by Classic Scan, Singapore
Printed by Times Offset (M) Sdn. Bhd.

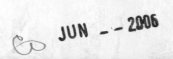

Contents

Introduction

Why do we read hands? It's a fascinating question, but the answer is simple: because we want to know about ourselves. We study our palms for the same reasons that people cast runes, read the Tarot, practise astrology or use other systems of divination. It's not just to look into the future; it's also to explore our personalities and emotions, to help us to understand our minds and talents and to see how we can become better people.

Palmistry is all about enhancing our lives. We can use it to see into existing situations, discover the reasons behind them and find the best way to make the most of them. The future is important, but if you believe that it is set in stone it will be a limited resource. We all have free will and are able to make our own decisions. Ideally, being able to read your palm will enable you to make the best choices and allow you to optimize your natural gifts and the opportunities that destiny brings your way.

Understand people

Your hand will also tell you about relationships, your health and why you react to life the way you do. Once you have mastered the art, it is fascinating to look at the hands of your friends and family. You may discover things about them you didn't realize. In fact, it's a good way of getting to know people.

Your hands are as unique as your fingerprints, but the lines on your hand change:

The lines of the hand

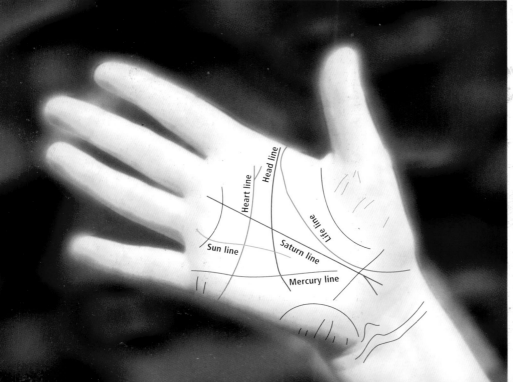

Heart line
Head line
Life line
Sun line
Saturn line
Mercury line

they appear, stretch, widen, shorten, disappear, grow longer, change colour and move around. They usually change slowly, at about the same rate as the lines on your face alter or your nails grow. These changes occur through the motions of the hands. Every time you bend a hand or finger a line is affected, and this is obvious when it comes to employment. If you start a driving job, for example, the way you hold the steering wheel and repeat certain actions, such as changing gear, will create new lines. Emotions and thoughts cause changes, too. We all move our hands subconsciously when we think, and that is why the lines of the palm express our emotions, aims and inner selves.

Left or right

The 'active' hand – right for right-hander, left for a left-hander – evolves more quickly because it is used more. The 'passive' hand – left for a right-hander, right for a left-hander – can become

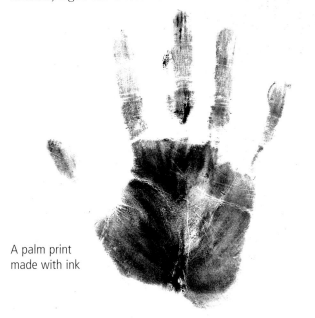

A palm print made with ink

Make a print of your hand

• Taking a handprint will reveal all the lines on your palm and is also useful if you have a friend who lives some distance away, who wants you to look at their palm. Making a handprint each year is a fascinating way of seeing how your lines are changing. They give you clues about how your personality is evolving and the ways in which your life is progressing.

• Handprints used to be taken with candle black. A clean sheet of paper was held over a candle flame and moved up and down, so that the carbon smoke from the candle formed a grey-black surface. The hand was pressed on to this to take a print. This method is excellent, although time consuming and messy, and these prints tend to smudge easily.

• It is easier to use a dark (black is best) water-based ink or paint. Have several sheets of white A4 (or foolscap) paper ready and sit at a sturdy table. Cover your hand thoroughly in ink, applying it with a roller, an old rag or a wad of cotton wool, and press it firmly on to the paper. Push down on the centre of the hand. It may take several goes to get the desired result. Most people have a slightly hollow Mars plain, which will not show on a print unless pressure is applied to the back of the hand. If all else fails, there's always the photocopier.

completely left behind or, if you are a busy person, lag only slightly behind the active hand.

The passive hand reveals the past, the essential you and how your personality is changing. The active hand, however, looks forwards to the future and shows how your character is growing and where you are going in life. It is best to focus on reading the active hand, but it is interesting to look at the passive hand afterwards and compare the two. This glimpse of how you were will reveal how much you have changed.

Where did palmistry come from?

The study of the hand is as old as mankind itself. So where did the idea originate? All mammals, marsupials, reptiles and birds take great pains about grooming themselves, and know every inch of their own bodies. Watch young animals, particularly birds, and you'll see them examine and poke at their feet with great interest. This is mirrored by the action of human babies, who often move their fingers around in front of their faces and watch them for hours.

During the Stone Age, people decorated their cave temples with unsurpassed artwork and hundreds of handprints, each of which signified that the person who had made it had been in the cave and taken part in the sacred mysteries.

Whatever its origins, palmistry was born of human curiosity. It would not have taken long before a Stone Age priest or priestess experienced a vision revealing that the strange markings on people's hands were put there to reveal secrets and map destinies. It would have become apparent that all were different but that all shared particular lines and markings. These were named and studied, becoming the head line, life line, fingerprints and so on.

Hand reading is common to most cultures around the globe but has especially deep roots in India and China, where ancient civilizations have long traditions of palmistry. Whether the different nations developed the idea and cross-fertilized each other or whether they invented the art in isolation is not known, but all palmistry traditions share common features.

The ancients

The practice of palmistry is recorded in ancient China, Babylon, Egypt, Persia, Greece, Rome and Tibet, and the system used by the Greek and Romans is the foundation of the one we use today. At first, palmistry was transmitted down the centuries by word of mouth, from teacher to pupil, and only later in writing.

The philosopher Aristotle (384–322BC), tutor to Alexander the Great, was a keen palmist, who passed his enthusiasm on to his pupils. Legend tells that he presented to Alexander an ancient scroll about palmistry that he found on an altar dedicated to the Greek god Hermes. Aristotle mentioned the lines of the hand in *De historia animalium*. It is believed that he wrote a major treatise on palmistry, which is now lost, although many later writers have tried to pass off their work as his.

The classical Greeks and Romans

It is said that when Aristotle had his hand read for the first time, his pupils were surprised that it showed so many signs of personality weakness.

Aristotle accepted the palmist's judgements, explaining that the faults shown were exactly the ones he had worked all his life to conquer.

Galen (129–c.199) was a Greek physician at the court of the Roman emperor, Marcus Aurelius and wrote on physiognomy, including material about the hand. The Roman poet and satirist Juvenal (55/60–c.127) explained how middle-class women consulted hand readers. The link between palmistry and astrology has always been strong, with planets, lines and mounts named after the same Roman gods. This system spread from Greece to Rome and may have reached Greece from Babylon, the reputed birthplace of astrology.

With the coming of Christianity, the occult arts, including palmistry, were often persecuted as pagan leftovers, and during the Middle Ages palmistry was left to witches and herbalists. However, it was championed by many pioneers of science, such as Paracelsus (1493–1541), the German alchemist and medical reformer, who used both astrology and palmistry in his work.

The nomadic gypsy tribes that wandered into Europe in the early fifteenth century popularized the art, but it was the invention of the printing press that made knowledge of the subject more readily available. The first book on palmistry was published in 1475.

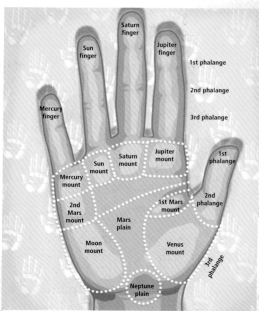

THE FINGERS AND MOUNTS

Writings by the Arabic physician Avicenna (980–1037) was translated for use in European medical colleges, complete with its hand and palm section. Between 1650 and 1730 palmistry was taught at the leading German universities.

In the nineteenth century two Frenchmen, Captain Stanilas d'Arpentigny and Adolphe Desbarrolles, provided the impetus for a renaissance in palmistry, lifting it from the disrepute into which it had fallen. D'Arpentigny made a life study of hand shapes and formulated their classification into seven main types. It is his system that forms the basis of the planetary system used in this book. His friend, Desbarrolles, worked as a practising palmist and he read for such luminaries as Napoleon III and Alexandre Dumas. His major contribution was to sort out which palmistry traditions he believed were based on truth and those which were merely superstitions. His book *Les Mystères de la main* was a turning point for it contained all the knowledge that was to be further refined by the next century's great palmists.

Today the future of palmistry is bright. Palmists are numerous, and scientists are using the study of the hand as a tool in psychology and as part of dermatoglyphics (the study of skin patterns) to pinpoint inherited diseases and even mental difficulties.

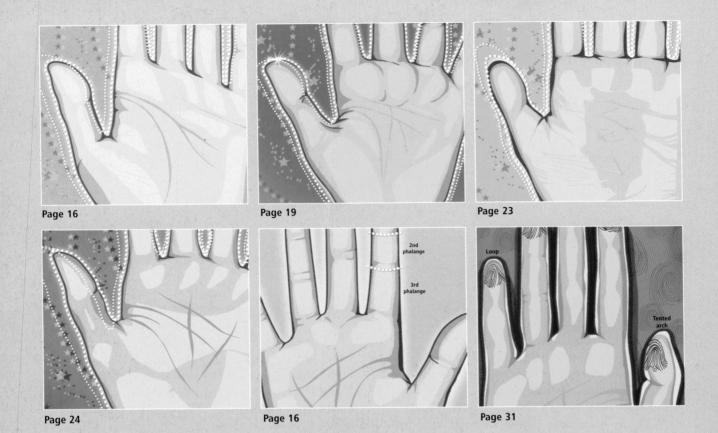

Page 16

Page 19

Page 23

Page 24

Page 16

Page 31

In this chapter you'll find out what sort of shape your hand is and what it means. Are you a sensitive person or a practical type? Do you think before you take action, or do you leap in? Look at the thumbnails above to see some of the different types of hand explained in this chapter. If you see one that resembles your hand, turn to that page and see what is revealed.

What Type Of Person Am I?

1

What Type Of Person Am I?

Your hands are as distinctive as your fingerprints. Although at first glance they may look like just another pair of hands, they are completely different from anyone else's.

The study of hand shapes was once considered to be a separate part of palmistry and was known as cheirognomy. Studying hand shapes is, in fact, even more important than reading the lines on the palm. The shape of your hand is the key to your personality; it is the face you show the world when you interact with other people and deal with the situations of daily life.

The planetary system

There are several systems for classifying hand shapes, but the oldest is the planetary system, which divides hands into seven types, each named after one of the planets of classical astrology: Mars, Venus, Moon, Mercury, Sun, Saturn and Jupiter. The hand shape named after Mars, for example, has the attributes associated with the planet Mars in astrology: fiery, radical, social and so on. Of course, not everyone falls into one of these seven categories, and many people are a combination of two shapes. With a little practice, you will be able to spot this and know if someone has a Mercury/Venus or a Saturn/Venus hand. If the hand is a mixed shape, the personality will be a combination of the two types, too. You will have to decide which shape is stronger and therefore will have more influence.

Fun with hand shapes

You can have a lot of fun with hand shapes. Once you have mastered the seven basic types, you can weigh up anyone you come into contact with, whether you are at work, at home or out and about socially. Just keep an eye on their hands, and without even asking them for a proper look you will be able to judge which shape their hand is – and then you'll know all about them.

To discover which hand shape you have, place your right hand on the illustrations you'll find on the next eight pages. When you have decided which shape fits your hand most closely, turn to the relevant page. It doesn't matter if you are left-handed because both your hands should be the same shape.

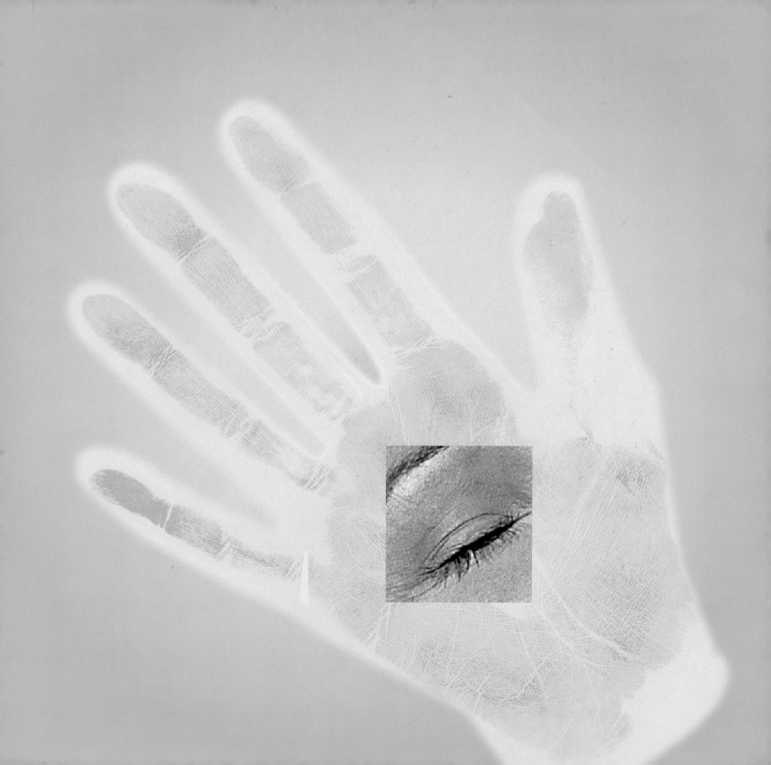

The Sun Hand

Sun-handed people are active, energetic achievers. They brim with confidence and launch into everything with gusto, never doing anything by halves. They are hard workers, and they often enjoy the physical exertion and mental stimulation their occupation provides.

Is my hand a Sun hand?

- Sun hands are alive with energy and power. They have a bold, round, muscular shape, and the fingers and nails are usually short, wide and strong. The thumb is heavy.
- All the mounts are raised, with the emphasis of strength in the mounts of Venus and Moon. The flesh is usually a vigorous red or pink. On the palm itself there are usually only a few lines, but these are deep and well marked.
- Sun hands are hot to the touch, and the skin is usually rough.
- The Roman sun god, Sol Invictus (the Invincible Sun), was linked to gold, fire, passion, victory and royalty.

They live life passionately and to the full, but they can overdo pleasure, sometimes eating or drinking too much. The family is important to Sun-handed people, as is a buzzing social life. Routine bores them, and challenge and change are necessities.

Hard workers

They make marvellous business people, always ready to work hard and use ideas to the full. They seize opportunities boldly and jettison unprofitable fields before others even sense downward trends. When they make mistakes, they can fall hard, but they soon recover, learning by experience.

Sun-handed people can be rash and overgenerous and spend money as fast as they make it. They indulge those they love and overlook others' shortcomings, often finding themselves used. Never push a Sun-handed person too far – they have troublesome tempers.

Fond of pleasure

Huge, robust Sun-handers are earthy, blunt, loving, and fond of simple pleasures. If the hand is hard, aggression, sexual dynamism and temper are present. Smaller, softer Sun hands are refined and witty conversationalists, who patronize the arts and love the company of creative people. They enjoy life's luxuries but can sometimes lack 'get up and go'. People with hard, large Sun hands revel in quantity and spiciness, both in their food and in life experience. Softer Sun hands are more gourmet-like and love sensual atmospheres. Both types are prone to overindulgence, whether it's with drink, gambling, sport, loving or working.

Sun-handers do well at practical occupations, such as construction, agriculture, crafts, financial services and the retail sector, and at anything that needs snap, intuitive decisions. More refined Sun-handers often find a niche in the arts or in a profession or business linked to them.

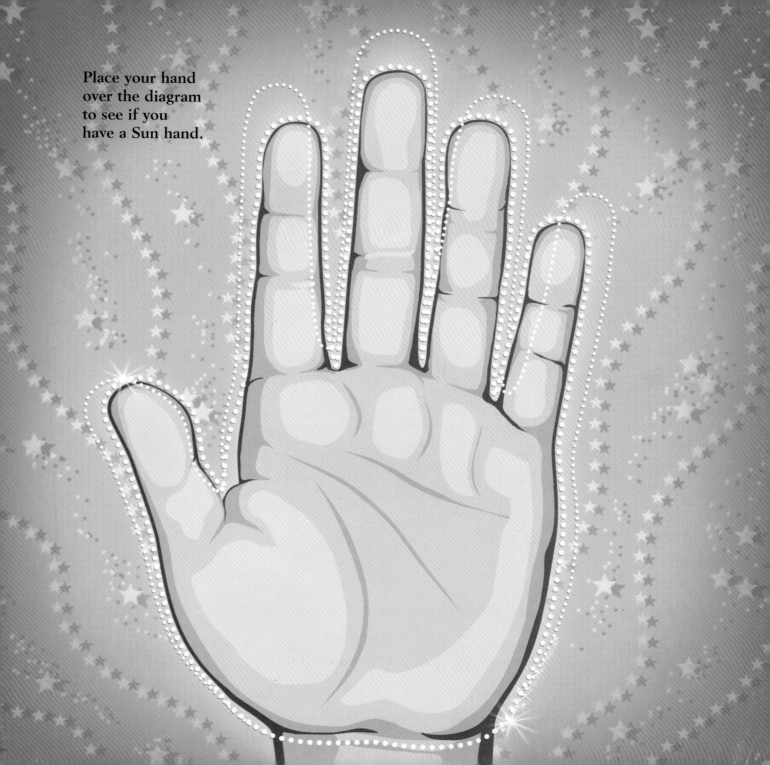

Place your hand over the diagram to see if you have a Sun hand.

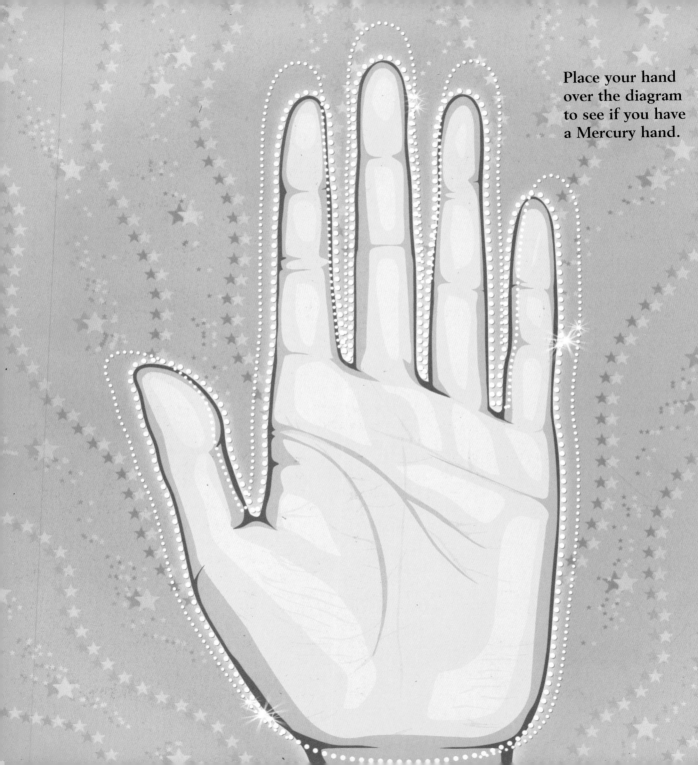

Place your hand over the diagram to see if you have a Mercury hand.

The Mercury hand

People with Mercury hands are brilliant communicators, both at work and home, and they love to talk, mix and mingle, knowing naturally how to spark a conversation. They have a nervous energy, which makes their minds work fast, and they crave self-expression. They instinctively master all communication techniques and are as happy e-mailing as chatting on the phone.

Is my hand a Mercury hand?

- Mercury hands are long and slender, and the basic shape of the palm is rectangular. The fingers, which are as long as the palm, join the palm in a sloping line, the Jupiter finger being set higher than the Saturn finger and so on. The fingers on some Mercury hands are set in a straight line, however, and this reveals the influence of Saturn and would make someone more down to earth and less highly strung.
- The skin is usually pale, and the palm is marked with many fine lines. Blue veins can often be seen below the porcelain skin.
- Mercury was the god of merchants, travellers, fortune-tellers, teachers and students, and he was associated with intelligence, communication, travel and business.

They can be nervous and lack confidence, but they are capable of great success in people-centred work. Career may not be their driving force, but the need to make a living stimulates their ambitions, and, once they get a taste for business or advancement in their chosen career, they do well. Self-employment offers exciting options. A literary or mathematical talent often backs up their quick wits and energy.

Sensitive ways

Mercury-handed people can lack perseverance and focus, escaping problems rather than tackling them. A finely tuned, sensitive nature means that a career can be sacrificed to workplace personality issues or troubles in their emotional life.

Socializing is important. Mercury-handers are the life and soul of the party. They are popular and romantic, often fickle in their younger days – understanding, communicative love partners are best for them.

A nervous nature

There is a tendency to nervousness, stress and worry. Relaxation and meditation can help to avoid psyche burn-outs. A natural flair for creativity and appreciation of the arts drives them to dress, spend and live well.

They love mystical subjects, being equally at home discussing astrology, alternative health therapies, meditation, psychoanalysis or whatever else allows them to explore their interest in the human mind. Anything new will grab their attention – for a while.

When the fingers of a Mercury hand join the palm in a straight line, Saturn's influence adds stamina and ability to help cope with routine.

Top Mercury career spheres include advertising, business, marketing, sales, travel, media, personnel and education.

The Mars hand

People with Mars hands are alive with restlessness, energy and eagerness. They are strongly individualistic, passionate about everything they do and can be impatient. They love to experiment and soon tire of routine, seeking fresh challenges and stimulation. The unknown is a constant draw.

Is my hand a Mars hand?

- There are two types of Mars hand, but the basic shape of each is the triangle. On some Mars hands the palm is wide below the fingers but tapers towards the wrist. On the other type the palm is wider above the wrist and grows narrower towards the fingers.
- Both types have the energy and idealism of Mars. Hands that are wider under the fingers are more practical; those that broader above the wrist are innovative and creative.
- Mars hands are usually pinkish or red in colour, and they tend to be hot to the touch.
- Most Mars-handed people have Mars fingers, too. They are rounded and bulbous at the end, like little spatulas.
- Mars was the Roman god of war, responsible for victory in battle and fertility.

Those with the first type of Mars hand – broad under the fingers – drive this enthusiasm into physical adventure or travel. The second type – the hand that is wider at the wrist – explore uncharted regions with their minds, innovating in science, medicine, design or technology, or seek to transform society and fight for justice. Both types are unafraid to go against the grain. More traditional minds may criticize and fight them, but Mars determination always triumphs.

Exciting lives

People with the first type of Mars hands enjoy being outdoors. They are suited to a military life, exploration, driving, diving, sports, agriculture, construction, engineering, demolition, rescue services and anything that calls for instant decisions and courage. Many find a career in education, health or politics or the social sector.

They succeed by refreshing tired concepts and launching new ones. If they do fail, they do it spectacularly but usually recover quickly.

Radical ideas

People with the second type of Mars hands are different. If the hand is soft they will be irritable and unsettled. Their challenge is to use their ideas and then stick with them.

Passions run wild in Mars hands. These people love deeply and physically, but are tender and caring, with strong family instincts. They fight loudly with their partners but forgive them easily.

Women with Mars hands are strong but feminine; men are masculine with a sensitive, caring side. Both men and women love sport.

When Mars hands are thwarted they suffer emotionally, becoming frustrated and angry. They need to find a way of releasing their feelings.

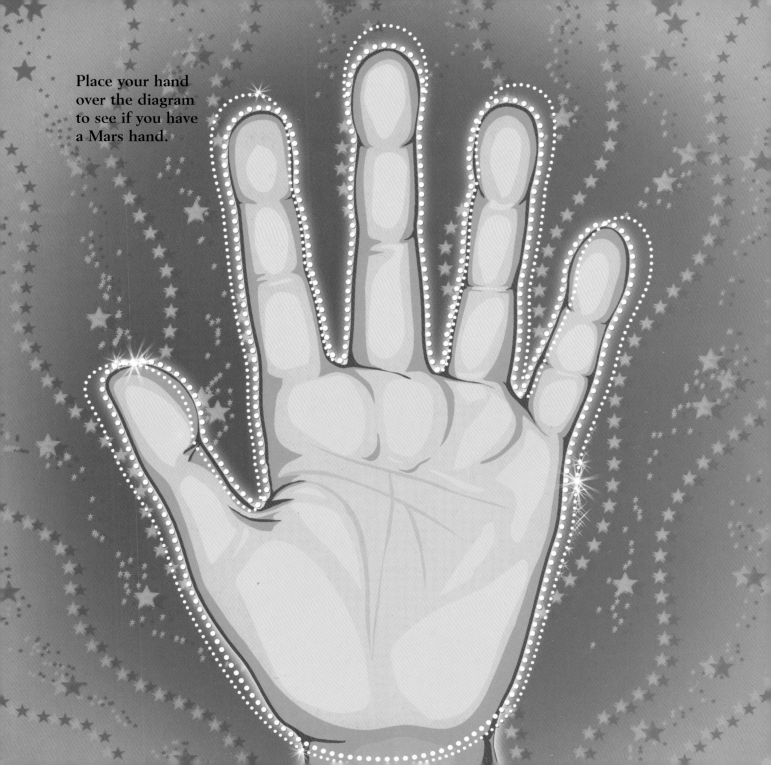

Place your hand over the diagram to see if you have a Mars hand.

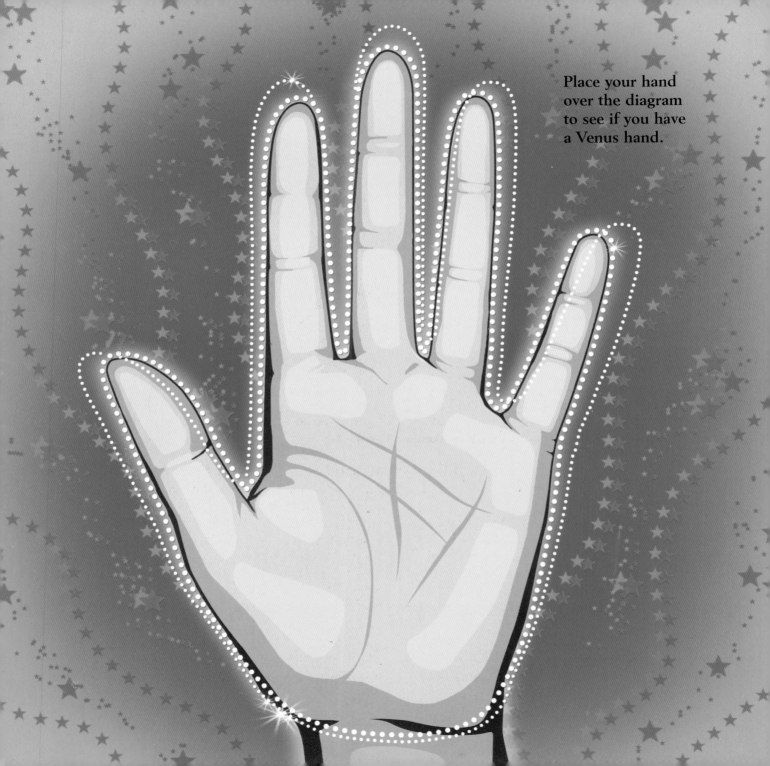

Place your hand over the diagram to see if you have a Venus hand.

The Venus hand

People with Venus hands love beauty and comfort, delighting in their expensive tastes and eating, drinking and living well, although happiness is more important to them. They feel at ease when they are surrounded by beautiful things.

Is my hand a Venus hand?

- Venus hands are graceful and refined, giving an instant impression of being attractive. The basic shape is oval, and all the curves of the hand are even and smoothly flowing.
- The mounts of the Moon and of Venus are usually the most powerful. The hand is firm but yielding and rarely hard.
- The fingers are well proportioned, wider but never too fat at the base. The fingertips are either gently rounded or slightly pointed.
- Venus hands are mostly pale in colour or are flushed with a delicate pink. The nails are always elegant, usually almond shaped, and they are well cared for.
- Venus, the Roman goddess of love, was associated with sensuality and the love of luxury and beauty.

A secure home environment is vital. It should be light and comfortable and house a well-loved pet or partner. Venus-handers have a talent for design, instinctively choosing the most appropriate outfits, hairstyles, home decors and garden layouts.

Powerful emotions

Venus hands could be called 'emotional hands', for they are dominated by feelings, impulses and sensitivities. Family and friends are top priorities. They can be fickle, falling in love with love itself and moving on when illusions are shattered. Each love disaster is a high drama, but they are attractive and soon recover when they find new partners.

They tend to be unambitious, but the firmer the hand the more success there will be in the chosen career. If they can focus, they excel in work that involves communicating with people, such as advertising, sales, the food industry, drama, beauty, hairdressing or fashion, personnel and recruitment. They can do well in humanitarian fields but must not become personally involved.

Creative and imaginitive

Vivid imaginations mean Venus handers daydream and flit from one interest to another. The arts and the glamorous aspects of psychic and alternative therapies attract them. They need self-discipline if they are to realize their creative potential.

They are naturally kind and giving, striving to see the best in everyone, and can be taken in by the less scrupulous. They could learn to be tougher and seek the truth about everyone and everything.

Most people with Venus hands have an excellent sense of intuition and a natural empathy with the emotions of others, sometimes becoming counsellors for their loved ones. Generous and popular, they thrive on good company.

The Saturn hand

People with Saturn hands possess tenacity and strength of will. They succeed through hard work; sensible, well-thought-out innovations and stamina. They plan ahead thoroughly.

Is my hand a Saturn hand?

- The palm of a pure Saturn hand is square. The fingers are arranged in a straight line, and the palm is square where it meets the wrist. Sometimes, even the fingers are square in shape, too. There are usually numerous, bold lines etched across the palm.
- The skin is a normal, healthy flesh tone with a hint of an earthy orange or pink. Saturn hands are dry to the touch and firm, rather than soft.
- Saturn was a Roman god of farming and culture. He was linked to the harvest of grain, and to time and the seasons, particularly the festivities known as the Saturnalia, traditionally celebrated from about 19 to 25 December, which later became Christmas.

They are traditional and reserved people, who love to persevere and fulfil their obligations to loved ones and society in general. They are rarely radical but have the discipline and patience to achieve their goals, as long as they are quick enough to seize useful opportunities. When they have a job or position that they feel benefits society, they are capable of great sacrifices.

Reliable and honest

Those with Saturn hands are reliable and tend to establish routines, but they are always open to change if it is advantageous.

Intrinsically honest, moral values and sincerity are important to them. They love religion and ceremony, often delving into mysticism.

They are survivors, able to turn to anything. Quick success is not important to them, but they cherish home values and stability. Although they can be patient, they fret while waiting. Underneath, there is great sensitivity, with a tendency to be easily hurt and to worry vigorously. They are as reliable emotionally as they are with life duties, capable of great sacrifice in relationships and feeling deep obligations to family and lovers.

Rhythmic

Gifted artists with Saturn hands are able to put their inspirations to practical use by bringing discipline to the creative process. Many successful composers, sculptors, musicians and poets have Saturn hands. People with Saturn hands love sacred and rhythmic music, and are natural linguists. Others find self-expression through gardening, breeding birds or animals, or writing.

They also excel in the arts, education, religion, health, translating, the law and government.

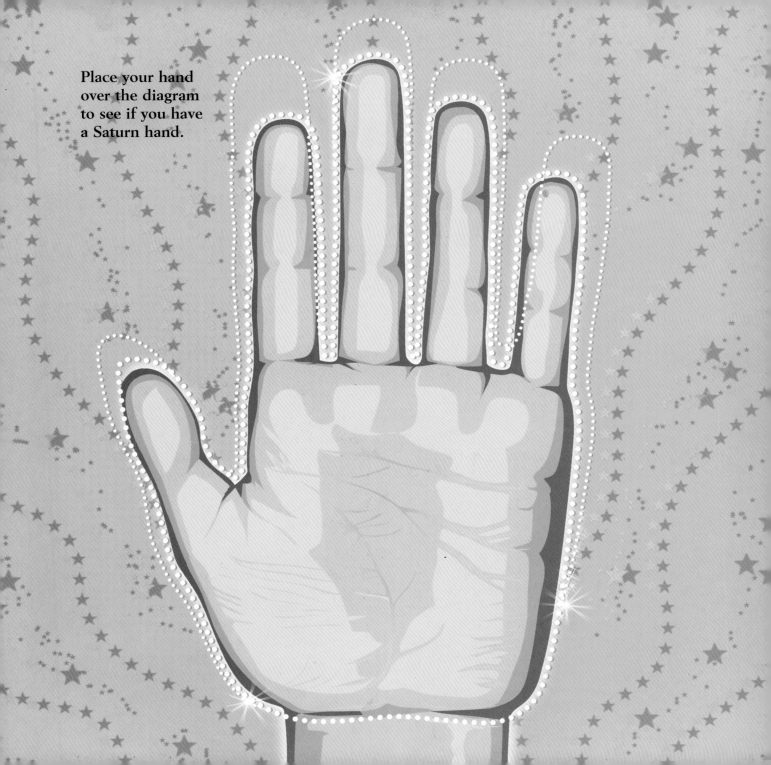

Place your hand over the diagram to see if you have a Saturn hand.

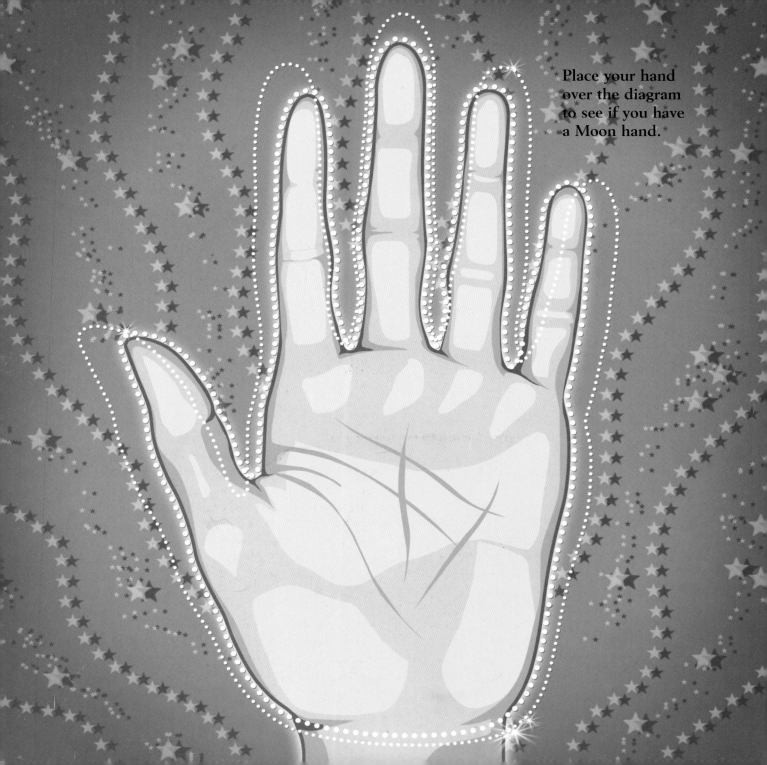

Place your hand over the diagram to see if you have a Moon hand.

The Moon hand

People with Moon hands are inquisitive and thoughtful and always highly strung. They are excellent communicators, with vivid imaginations and active fantasy lives. At their worst, they are selfish, self-absorbed and inclined to paranoia. They can become withdrawn and generally remain a little aloof.

Is my hand a Moon hand?

- The Moon hand is one of the rarer hand shapes. It is almost like a figure-of-eight and tends to be flat and long with prominent veins and a depressed Mars plain. The hand gives an overall impression of being elongated and bony, even awkward. The fingers and nails are long, and the knuckles are large.
- The skin is always pale, sometimes with blue or grey tints. It is often cold and has either a waxy or a dry texture.
- The Romans worshipped the Moon goddess as either Luna or Diana. She was patroness of women, witches, childbirth, magic, hunting and animals.

This is not a practical hand. People with Moon hands are thinkers and dreamers, analyzing every facet of life and sifting facts and feelings to extract precise truths. They have a desperate need to know. At a lower level this causes nosiness; at a higher, however, it draws them to philosophy, mysticism and religion. It is in these areas that they often make their mark.

Gifted imagination

Moon handers have strong imaginations and perceptive minds, often turning their talents to improving the lives of others, but they can be ruthless in pursuit of goals. They have a capacity for extreme self-denial and sacrifice. They are at their best when they can afford to be philanthropic and champion artistic, spiritual or political causes.

They can be selfish and introverted, demanding attention and trying to be different. Ambition takes the form of acquiring respect or authority in a difficult field. They crave recognition for creativity, intelligence or achievement. Money and material possessions hold little attraction.

Intuition

These people make eloquent public speakers, intuitively understanding the mind of their audience and controlling it. This suits them for religion, education, psychology, psychiatry, counselling, politics, leisure and the arts or for jobs as receptionists, secretaries, administrators or community workers.

They can become withdrawn and love solitude, or they can thrive on being among and observing people, sometimes alternating between the two, depending on their mood.

There is a tendency for Moon-handed people to become set in their ways, causing them to become stuck in negative situations, escaping in their imaginations rather than in reality.

The Jupiter hand

A Jupiter hand can be the best or worst of the six shapes. People with Jupiter hands are flexible, adapting readily to any situation, quickly mastering the skills essential to survival and prosperity and becoming more Martian, Venusian and so on as required.

Is my hand a Jupiter hand?

- Jupiter hands are hard to define because they are a combination of all the other hand shapes. Any hand that seems to take its attributes from three or more of the hand shapes is a Jupiter hand.
- Typical Jupiter hands are broad rather than long, pink and warm to the touch. The thumb is longish and all the fingers are of different planetary types (see Chapter 2). Usually, the Jupiter finger has a Venus fingertip, the Saturn finger has a Saturn fingertip, the Sun finger has a Mars fingertip, while the Mercury finger has a Mercury fingertip.
- Jupiter was the king of the gods, and the father of most of them.

A strong Jupiter hand – heavy and robust, firm fleshed with powerful mounts and a deep head line – usually succeeds, no matter what comes their way. Someone with a weak Jupiter hand, with a hollow palm, low mounts and pale skin, has a worrying, fussing, easily led and never satisfied nature. Such people tend to lack direction and often drift from one thing to another, job to job and place to place, just getting by.

Generous but self-indulgent

Most people with Jupiter hands are generous and sometimes self-indulgent; all are sociable and popular. Although they like to control their own destiny and gain status, they are magnanimous and fair.

People with Jupiter hands are survivors, who can adapt to any circumstances. They fit anywhere, finding talents for the most diverse things. They jump careers with ease, designing theatre backdrops one minute and selling insurance the next. They find friends in any social circle, drinking with sports fans at lunch and dining with the in-crowd at night.

Talented but changeable

They are changeable people, dropping projects on a whim and brimming with ideas. Brilliant conversationalists, they excel in work that requires diplomacy and tact when dealing with others.

They are instinctively fine business people, but they love to spend and gamble. Their challenge is to stick at one thing. They also enjoy the arts, finding they can sing, act or dance, but they will need perseverance to ever shine.

These people do best in the leisure industry, travel and maintenance or in anything where a wide range of qualities and skills are called for.

Place your hand
over the diagram
to see if you have
a Jupiter hand.

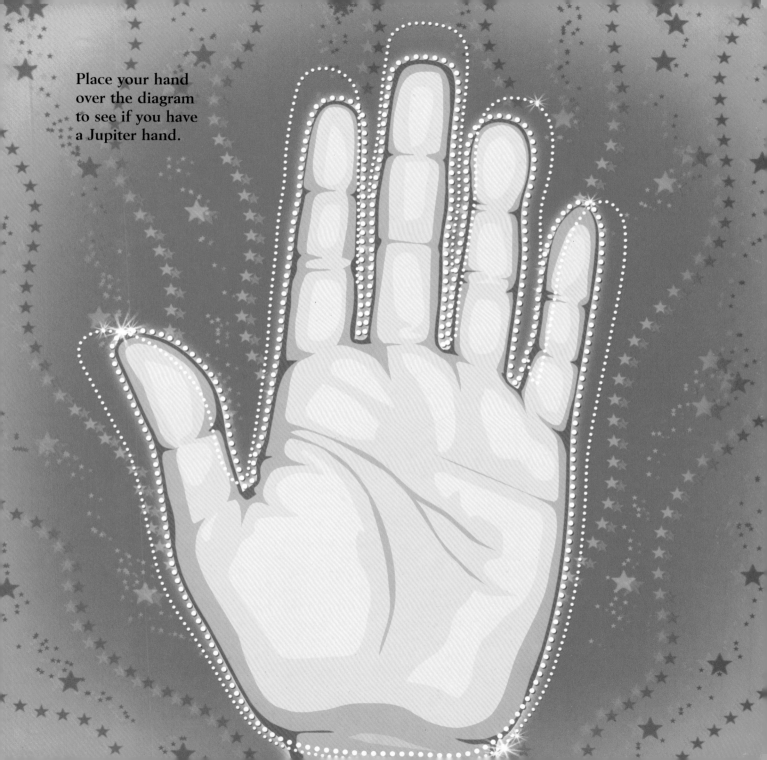

What do my fingers tell me about myself?

Like the hands, each finger is named after one of the planets of astrology: Jupiter, Saturn, the Sun (which, in astrology, is counted as a planet) and Mercury. Each is divided into three phalanges. The first phalange is the fingertip, the second phalange is below the first knuckle, and the third is between the second knuckle and the palm.

The forefinger, named the Jupiter finger, relates to ambition, self-esteem and leadership qualities. The middle finger, the Saturn finger, denotes duty, tradition and sense of time. The ring finger relates to success, creativity and sociability. The little finger or the Mercury finger, links to communication talents, wit and an ability to influence others.

Long or short fingers

The relative length and strength of each finger must be weighed up to assess the power of its attributes. For instance, a normally proportioned Jupiter finger signifies confidence, average organizational abilities and healthy ambition.

The Jupiter finger is usually half a fingertip shorter than the Saturn finger. An extremely well-developed Jupiter finger denotes a desire for power, burning ambition, a tendency to bossiness and towering self-opinion. If it is weak and insignificant, it shows a lack of willpower, damaged self-esteem and a lack of motivation. A long Jupiter finger betrays a power-at-all-costs attitude, immense pride and the attitude of a dictator or evangelist.

The Saturn finger is generally the longest. If overdeveloped it emphasizes the planet Saturn's restrictive character, bringing depressive tendencies, introspection, submission to fate and a vision of life as a duty-filled burden. When under-formed and weak, especially if the tip is pointed, it denotes a careless and irresponsible nature that lacks the willpower to improve itself.

Ambitious or shy

The Sun finger is usually slightly shorter and slimmer than the Jupiter finger. If the Sun finger is as long and as strong as the Jupiter finger, there will be a love of people, romance, life and creative tendencies, and a desire for the fame and money associated with media or artistic success. A weak or short Sun finger speaks of a shy, retiring personality, one that is timid and repressed. When the Sun finger is exceptionally long, its owner will be a gambler and seek to live life to the full, indulging a love of risk taking and a powerful sexual drive.

The Mercury finger normally reaches nearly to the base of the Sun finger's first phalange. The longer the Mercury finger, the more eloquent and persuasive its possessor. A noticeably long Mercury finger reflects skill in communication, a linguist, writer, politician, philosopher or a leader, who can influence others and attract followers. If this finger is short, communication skills will be lacking, and thoughts and feelings remain unexpressed. A crooked Mercury finger makes self-expression difficult. When it is bent round like a claw, its owner's personality is often introverted and perhaps even sullen.

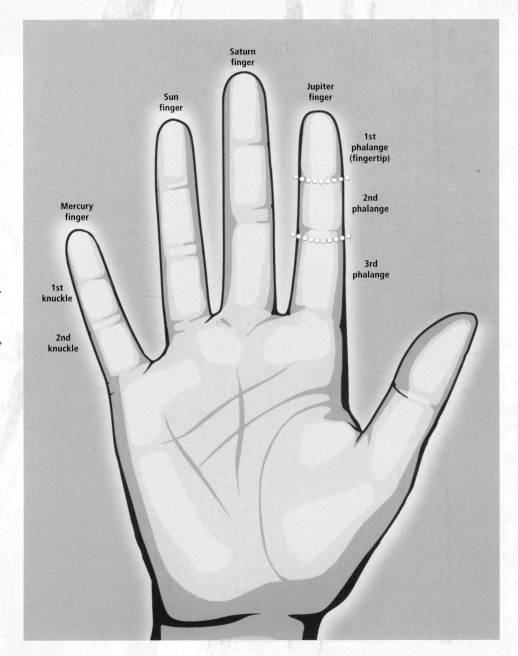

What do my fingerprints reveal about me?

Fingerprints reveal the personality traits that you were born with and that were passed on to you genetically. If possible, check your parents hands and see whose are more like yours.

Take a look at your hand and you'll see the head, heart and life lines. Beneath these are thousands of finer lines, flowing across the palm in swirling patterns. These can be seen best in strong light or under a magnifying glass. They are known as skin ridges, and they cover both hands and fingers. Everyone has completely individual skin ridge and fingerprint patterns, and their most fascinating use is in the identification of suspects through prints left at crime scenes.

Loop, tent, arch or whorl

The fingerprints illustrated on this page are examples of the five types: arch, tented arch, whorl, loop and composite. Compare your own fingerprints with them. If one of your fingerprints seems to be a blend of two, the characteristics it displays will be a combination of those associated with the two types. If one predominates, so will its traits. Bear in mind that 65 per cent of all human fingerprints are loops.

Inner life/outer life

The fingerprints on the active hand – right for a right-hander, left for a left-hander – show how we cope with life, our attitudes and the way we achieve our potential. Those on the passive hand – left for a right-hander, right for a left-hander – express our inner selves and our reactions to emotional situations, family and home life.

Look at every finger and count how many of each fingerprint type there are. Jot your count down on paper if it helps. Then count the types of fingerprint on each hand. Sometimes the balance is the same for right and left hands. If not, it signifies that your inner life differs from your public face.

Yin or yang?

• Traditional Japanese and Chinese palmists consider that only whorl fingerprints are yang and positive, while all others are yin and negative. Whorl fingerprints do mark energy and radicalism.

ARCHES

A majority of arch fingerprints indicates people who are traditional, responsible, honest and usually contented. They like to conform and appreciate simple things and pleasures, but they can be inflexible, restrictive, proud and not good at coping with pressure. They prefer to stick with familiar faces and things, have trouble with self-expression and lack spontaneity.

TENTED ARCHES

People with a majority of tented arch fingerprints are enthusiastic, warm and sincere. They are devoted and committed, emotional, idealistic and campaigning. They are also creative, appreciating the arts and music, sensitive and highly strung with intense inner lives.

Both arch and tented arch fingerprints indicate people who love tradition, revere family values and, whether liberal minded and creative or not, seem old fashioned.

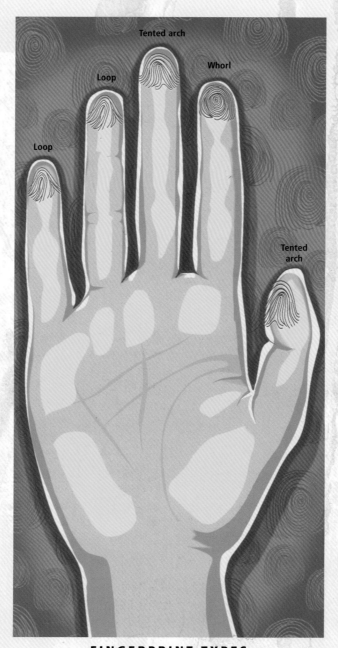

FINGERPRINT TYPES

LOOPS

People who have a majority of loop fingerprints are open-minded, accepting and willing to experiment. They tend to be self-assured, flexible and communicative, and they are social reformers, sympathetic and practical. They are responsive emotionally but can lack focus.

COMPOSITES

A majority of composite fingerprints indicate people who are diplomatic, hesitant and receptive to both sides of an argument. They are balanced, willing to live and let live and happy to please everyone, but they may be resentful. These people are earthy, realistic, practical but idealistic, and they can become muddled.

WHORLS

A majority of whorls suggests people who are confident, strong willed, ambitious, and driven. Such people are individualistic, self-interested and stubborn, but they are also original and iconoclastic. They may be secretive, not easily trusting and eager for privacy.

The fingerprints

Each fingerprint needs to be read individually, too. The majority of thumb and Mercury fingerprints are loops, so any deviation from this is a powerful indicator. In addition, if the Jupiter finger or any other on the active hand differs from the fingerprint on the passive hand, it suggests significant differences between inner and outer lives. Interpret the following as relating to attitudes and actions if they are on the active hand, and to emotions and relationships if they are on the passive hand.

ON THE THUMB

• Arch: set in ways; a tendency to categorize people; stubborn; practical; constructs a traditional life.
• Tented arch: determined but reasonable; devoted; willing to fight for justice.
• Loop: expressive; knows own mind and is self-assured; able to work in partnerships or teams while keeping own aims intact; avoids conflict; diplomatic.
• Composite: hesitant and unsure of self; will not fight for beliefs.
• Whorl: immense willpower; extremely persistent; focused; will fight to win.

ON THE JUPITER FINGER

• Arch: content with limited social circle; unambitious but hard-working; trustworthy; courageous; copes with anything.
• Tented arch: enthusiastic; committed; champions causes; excellent career; caring for people or animals.

• Loop: good at problem-solving and people skills; fine administrator; copes well with everyday life.
• Composite: able to understand all sides of an argument; excels in the fields of legal work, arbitration or diplomacy.
• Whorl: excellent communicator; best working on own initiative; often found in caring environments; high self-esteem but sensitive; strongly goal orientated. A whorl on both Jupiter fingers indicates that there is a vocation or destiny in one particular life role, which includes a need to help others and to feel useful within the community. There is a strong urge to be best or even to be unique in the chosen field.

ON THE SATURN FINGER

• Arch: desires attention; easily flattered; pompous; pragmatic about spirituality; follows a religion if it improves quality of life.
• Tented arch: enthusiastically embraces religions, issue politics or movements.
• Loop: open minded about spirituality or

mystical viewpoints; well versed in a wide range of subjects; inquiring mind.

• Composite: mystical yet practical, imaginative, capable, balances spiritual and material needs.

• Whorl: knows own mind; follows own agenda and morality; self-believing; strong philosophical ideals; judgmental; can hold unorthodox religious or spiritual ideas; exceptionally good at carrying out innovative research.

ON THE SUN FINGER

• Arch: conforming; fits in with family or social environment; moralistic.

• Tented arch: gift for music; a sense of rhythm; poetic; capable of lateral thought.

• Loop: quick to adapt to changes in society or other people's needs; follower of fashion; appreciates innovations as long as they conform to own ideas of beauty and harmony.

• Composite: loving with intimates and friends; disinterested in outsiders; practical and tough.

• Whorl: Creative; artistic; individualistic; usually eccentric; seeks an audience; loves applause.

ON THE MERCURY FINGER

• Arch: poor communication skills; introverted; always follows proper channels.

• Tented arch: talented speaker; persuasive; loves to be heard and to express own views.

• Loop: fine talker; freely expressive; projects warmth and humour; gets along with most people; has a knack for teamwork.

• Composite: sometimes vocal and sociable, sometimes withdrawn; capable of expressing two diverse opinions; blunt.

• Whorl: sincere; dedicated; talks with forceful passion; promotes or defends beliefs with conviction; speech is focused, never trivial or wasteful; marvellous organizer; takes great pains over detail; a perfectionist.

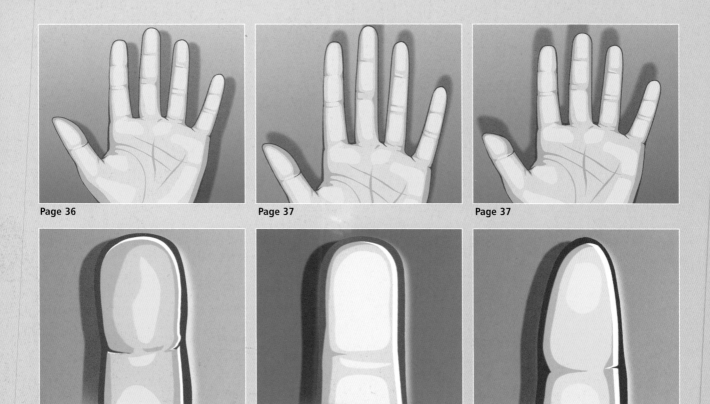

Page 36

Page 37

Page 37

Page 40

Page 41

Page 41

Your fingers are the gateways to self-expression. Have you got a way with words or are you shy and retiring? In this chapter you can pinpoint what shape fingers you have, whether they're long or short, and discover what this says about you. The pictures above show some of the finger shapes you'll find in this chapter. Turn the pages to find out which ones you have.

How Do I Express Myself?

2

How Do I Express Myself?

The shape of our hands reveals what type of people we are, but we don't always express our true selves when we relate to others. It is our fingers that show how we connect to the world.

Our fingers are vital to us. With the thumb, they allow us to do all the things that make our lives special, such as cooking, dressing, holding tools and expressing affection. They flutter and point during conversation, showing our feelings.

Fingers express our thoughts and emotions, and through their motions they create the lines on the palm. The more someone's fingers move when they talk, the more highly strung they are and the quicker their mind works. When the fingers are clenched as if a fist is being made, they indicate anger or the repression of that individual's true opinion.

AVERAGE HAND
Fingers and palm the same length

Are my fingers long?

• Consider your fingers in relation to your hand size. A long hand usually has long fingers, but they are considered 'long' only if they are long in proportion to the palm. A Saturn finger longer than the palm means you have long fingers.

LONG FINGERS

The longer someone's fingers are, the more sensitive and highly strung they will be. People with long fingers take account of the thoughts and emotions of others, and they are cautious about what they say. Their communication skills are heightened, but they can be timid and are easily upset, even if they don't show it.

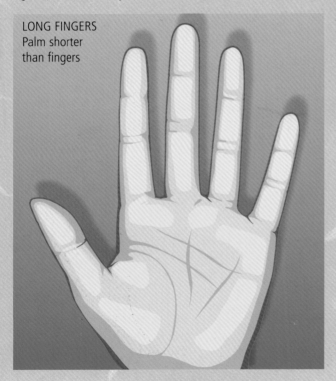

LONG FINGERS
Palm shorter
than fingers

SHORT FINGERS
Fingers shorter
than palm

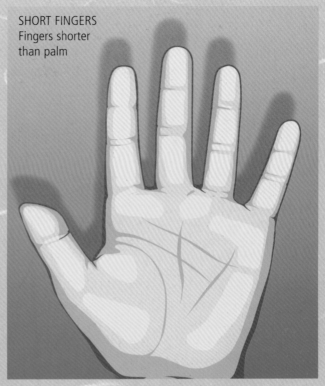

Are my fingers short?

• If the length of your Saturn finger is noticeably shorter than the length of your palm, you have short fingers.

SHORT FINGERS

Short fingers mark an impulsive nature, which bases decisions and responses on instinct and whims. People with short fingers are blunt and say whatever they like, because they care little for the concerns and feelings of others or for what society thinks. The shorter the fingers are, the more impulsive the character.

Thick fingers or thin?

Thick fingers look thick when they are judged by the proportions of the rest of the hand, and vice versa for thin fingers.

THIN FINGERS

Thin fingers signify refined tastes, nervousness and self-consciousness, and they can indicate a lack of energy or motivation. People with thin fingers will enjoy discussing anything they consider intelligent or creative, but they will not like vulgar humour or subjects that aren't politically correct.

THICK FINGERS

Thick fingers show coarser tastes, and people with thick fingers will thrive on talking about the basic pleasures of life, food, sex, drink and so on. They enjoy a good laugh and sometimes revel in having fun at other people's expense.

How do your knuckles affect your conversation?

The knuckles are the joints between the phalanges. They affect speed of thought and how much consideration is given to what is said. Most people's knuckles fall between the two extremes.

BIG KNUCKLES

People with big knuckles pay attention to details. They say what they mean and take pains to explain things properly. They are inquisitive and ask lots of questions, but do like to find things out for themselves, so they don't always believe what they are told. They make good listeners.

SMOOTH JOINTS

Smooth-jointed people are as impulsive with their words as they are with their thoughts and actions. They say whatever comes into their heads and go off at a tangent, which can be amusing. They get impatient with long-winded talkers, love to laugh and are useless at remembering details.

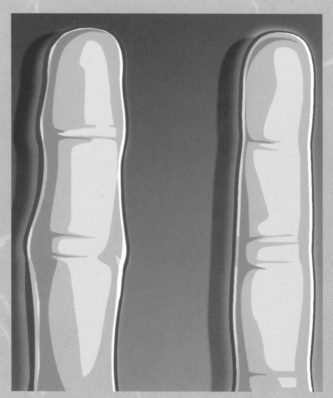

Big knuckles   Smooth joints

What type of fingertips have I got?

Fingertips come in various shapes. Sometimes all four on a hand are the same, but they may all be different. The basic fingertip shapes are named after the astrological planets in the same way that the hand shapes and fingers are. To find out what fingertip shapes you have, place your fingertips on the illustrations of Venus and Saturn fingertips (below) and see which one is the best fit.

VENUS FINGERTIPS

Venus fingertips are oval, graceful and refined. They mark a person who is idealistic, romantic and tasteful, loves beauty, hates coarseness and searches for the best in people. Those with Venus fingertips enjoy discussing culture, TV, films, fashion and will have an intense interest in all aspects of life. They have a kind word for everybody and don't like conversations that profoundly challenge their ideas.

SATURN FINGERTIPS

Saturn fingertips are square. They reflect someone who is sensible, practical and methodical in their speech. People with Saturn fingertips are true to their word, patient and thoughtful. They take things seriously, love being useful and tend to worry about what others think of them because they like to make a good impression. They often find themselves giving advice.

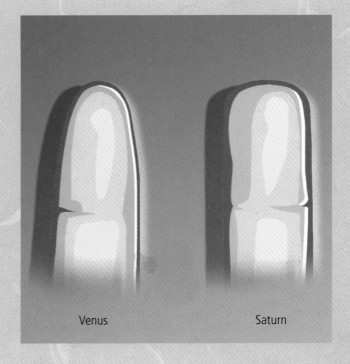

Venus   Saturn

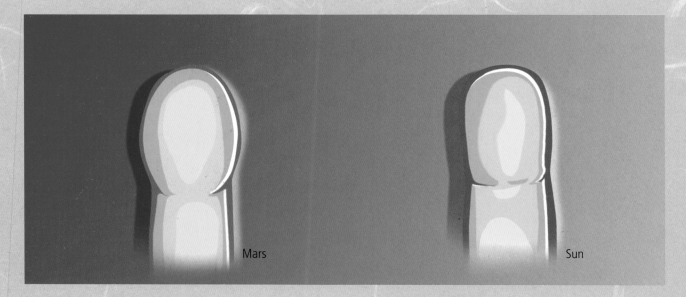

Mars

Sun

MARS FINGERTIPS

Mars fingertips bulge out from the finger like little spoons or spatulas. They point to a nature that is original, expressive, eccentric, passionate, enthusiastic and innovating. People with Mars fingertips are unafraid to experiment and are always busy. They talk fast and enjoy debate and discussion, and they also display an excellent sense of humour. If the company is too serious or not lively enough, they get frustrated, and may try to 'get things going' by beginning an argument or saying something outrageous.

SUN FINGERTIPS

Sun fingertips are large, robust and round, indicating a lust for life, enjoyment of physical pleasures and vibrant health. People with these fingertips love to be the centre of attention, and have always got something to say. If they are not active or admired, they become bored and restless.

MOON FINGERTIPS

Moon fingertips are wide, pale, rounded and quite flat. They reveal thoughtfulness, a nervous streak and a vivid imagination. People with Moon fingertips often have religious or philosophical leanings, and they may have a weak constitution. When they are in a crowd they can be a little shy, even introverted, although on another occasions they seek attention. They also exaggerate for effect.

MERCURY FINGERTIPS

Mercury fingertips are thin and almost pointed. They mirror a mind that is trusting, sensitive, sometimes highly strung, intuitive and in tune with what is happening around them. People with these fingertips are empathetic with others and are better at sorting out other people's problems than their own. They love to talk and will discuss anything, being brilliant at putting information across in the best way possible.

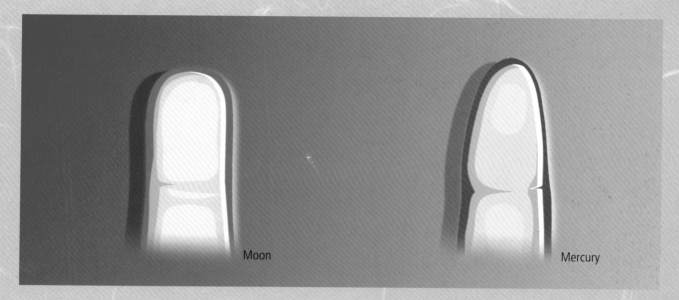

Moon

Mercury

JUPITER FINGERTIPS

Jupiter fingertips are simply fingertips that fail to match any of the other categories. They give clues of a changeable personality, capable of being all things to all men and able to transform itself as the need arises. These people are excellent communicators, fitting in with any crowd and finding something to say on every topic.

COMBINATIONS

The attributes connected to the planetary fingertip shapes are not set in stone, and the art is to relate them to the seven planetary hand shapes. This is straightforward when we find a Mars hand with Mars fingertips – the sign of a typical fiery, passionate Mars personality – but it is more complicated when the fingertips do not match the hand shape. All combinations can be worked out as long as you remember that the hand shape symbolizes the core energy of the personality, while the fingertip shapes give clues about how that energy is expressed and perceived in the world.

For example, a Mars hand with Saturn fingertips suggests that the energetic ways of Mars are restricted by Saturn's sobering influence. Such a person would not put their ideas into practice straightaway. They would research them thoroughly and act at the correct time. Many of their passions would remain unexpressed and their general nature would be more considerate and thoughtful than is usually associated with Mars.

It is also common to find a hand bearing four different fingertip types. Usually there is a Venus tip on the Jupiter finger, a Saturn tip on the Saturn finger, a Mars or Sun tip on the Sun finger, and a Mercury tip on the Mercury finger. This points to a balanced personality, with the energies of each finger complimented by their fingertips, the Venus fingertip softening and balancing Jupiter's strength.

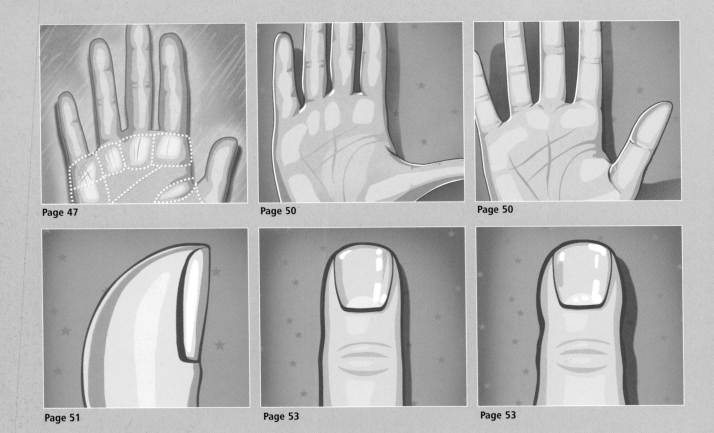

Page 47

Page 50

Page 50

Page 51

Page 53

Page 53

Here, you can explore your inner drives. Are you motivated by a sense of justice, or do you resist change? Does the environment concern you, or are you motivated purely by success? The thumb, parts of the fingers and the mounts, reveal your qualities, good and bad, progressive and reactionary.

What Are My Strengths?

3

What Are My Strengths?

It is essential that we know what our natural talents and characteristics are. Once we do, we can promote our strengths and strive to eradicate or overcome our weaknesses. Fortunately, the things we consider our strengths, whether they are sports or intellectual pursuits, are normally our favourite activities. It is even more fortunate if we can find work or a profession that allows our natural talents and aptitudes to blossom.

The contours of the palm are known as mounts and plains. Their height or depth, firmness or softness paint a revealing picture of our strengths. The eight mounts and two plains are named after the planets of astrology. Study the illustration and then your hand, looking at the relative heights and depths of each mount.

Note which mount is the most powerful, because it is this one that will dominate your character. Usually it is the Jupiter, Venus or the Moon mount that is prominent. Sometimes two mounts predominate, which means that their combined personality traits determine your nature.

A raised mount is stronger than usual. The more it is raised, the stronger it is. If a mount is barely present, the characteristics it represents will be compromised. The harder it is, the more forcefully its powers will be used in the world. The softer it is, the less its qualities will be utilized. A firm, medium mount has a more positive effect on someone's life path than a large, flaccid one.

On an ideal hand, all the mounts are well formed, slightly raised and firm but not too hard.

Such a hand would represent a person with a completely balanced character.

If a mount is strong its powers are well developed. If it is weak they are barely adequate and if it is overdeveloped they can be taken too far. Should a mount be absent altogether, its strengths are lacking. Sometimes there will be a dip in the palm's surface instead of a mount, and where this happens that mount's gifts are reversed – tactfulness becomes bluntness and so on.

JUPITER MOUNT

The Jupiter mount grants ambition, a willingness to experiment, leadership ability, pride and egotism. It also signifies a sense of honour and justice, generosity, benevolence, pomposity, self-indulgence, concentration, enthusiasm and a religious instinct.

SATURN MOUNT

This mount emphasizes a love of the natural world, an understanding of time, a belief in fate, fatalism and a passion for mysticism or the occult. It also indicates responsibility, a firm sense of duty, a love of tradition, cynicism, restrictive attitudes, a powerful sense of rhythm, an appreciation of music, a liking for solitude, caution, financial astuteness and a fondness for work.

SUN MOUNT

The Sun mount shines with a love of life, laughter and company. It signifies spontaneity, grace, creative talent, success and the ability to win celebrity, and an aptitude for the comic, intuition, versatility, flexibility, egotism, artistic appreciation, charisma and attention-seeking ways.

MERCURY MOUNT

This mount gives business ability, high powers of self-expression and excellent communication skills. It suggests natural diplomacy and a flair for negotiation, as well as educational aptitude, a sense of humour, adaptability, nervous energy, eloquence, a sharp critical faculty and a love of travel and change.

MOON MOUNT

The Moon mount gifts good taste and a sense of colour, refinement and imagination. It indicates inspiration, creativity and skills in poetry and writing, as well as a mystical, idealist outlook, a deep spiritual bond with nature and superstitious beliefs. It also shows selfishness, a weak sense of reality, laziness and a low boredom threshold.

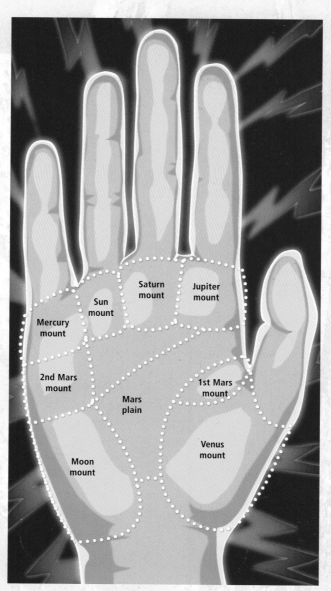

THE MOUNTS AND MARS PLAIN

VENUS MOUNT

A raised Venus mount ensures generousity, personal warmth and a strong sexuality and sensuality in its owner. It suggests an ability to empathize and sympathize, a caring attitude, an instinctive appreciation of nature, love and beauty, a joyful outlook and helpful ways. However, there may also be a tendency towards self-indulgence.

MARS MOUNTS

The first Mars mount gives great courage, a willingness to defend or protect, a readiness to take offence, a fighting spirit, a temper, a sense of honour, patriotism and loyalty.

The second Mars mount reveals a firm community spirit, self-control, a sense of justice, social awareness, morality, a resignation to burdens and responsibilities, political talent and ambition.

MARS PLAIN

The Mars plain should be flat rather than raised like a well-formed mount. Examine and feel yours. Is it level or raised, low or dipped, firm or soft?

A LEVEL MARS PLAIN

The ideal Mars plain is level or slightly raised and it should be firm, a healthy colour and with few lines crossing it. Such a plain would show someone who is peace-loving, diplomatic and ready to give others the benefit of the doubt but who is quick to react when required, eager to express themselves, ready to stand up in their own defence or that of anyone else deserving protection, and determined when required.

A HIGH MARS PLAIN

The higher the Mars plain stands from the hand, the quicker and more furious the temper. In extreme cases, aggressiveness and the capability for violence are shown. Fine or red lines on this plain makes the temper worse.

A HOLLOW MARS PLAIN

If the plain takes the form of a hollow, the lower it sinks, the weaker, more melancholy and more lacking in spirit its owner is. Inability to make decisions, nervousness, low self-esteem and lack of confidence would be problems. Such people repeat bad life choices, become stuck in cycles and invariably blame their 'luck' – anything except themselves.

Mars, Mars, Mars

The first Mars mount, the second Mars mount and the Mars plain all express different aspects of Mars' energies. The first Mars mount relates to Mars as the warrior, the second to Mars as the leader, lawmaker and enforcer, while the Mars plain determines how these impulses are acted on.

A SOFT MARS PLAIN

The softer the Mars plain, the more the character becomes dithering, nervous, worried and easily influenced by stronger personalities. Such people are incapable of sticking up for themselves, of forming a solid opinion or of making a decision.

A HARD MARS PLAIN

The harder or firmer the plain, the more powerful the strength of will. Such people are able to analyse data, form opinions and take the lead and express their ideas and feelings. They act as an individual, are confident and have self-belief.

What else should I look out for?

The strengths of the mounts are effected by the lines on them and by any other markings or blemishes.

WHAT IF I HAVE LINES ON MY MOUNTS?

A single, deep, vertical line travelling down a mount strengthens it. Two lines increase its power to a lesser extent. Three lines boost its energies, but not as highly as two lines. If there are more than three lines, the mount's effectiveness begins to diminish. If there are many lines, especially if there are also horizontal ones, the mount's negative traits are brought out.

WHAT IF MY MOUNTS AREN'T IN THE RIGHT PLACE?

The qualities of an out-of-place mount – for instance, a Jupiter mount close to the Saturn mount – are influenced by those of the other mount. Jupiter's ambition would be restricted by Saturn's sense of duty, for example. If a mount is near to a more powerful mount, the weaker would be sublimated.

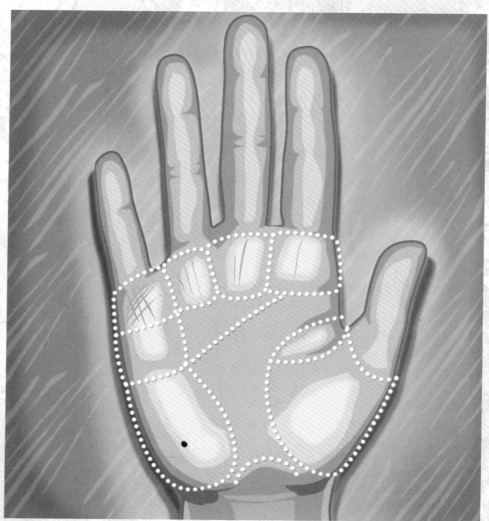

Marks on the mounts

DOES IT MATTER IF I'VE A CALLUS ON A MOUNT?

Calluses on a mount are significant, and it is not just manual workers who have these blemishes. A callus is a layer or lump of hardened skin, formed by the body as a protection against constant pressure. A gardener who digs all day will grow calluses on one or two of his mounts. However, they can just as easily occur through driving, housework or playing golf. On an inner level they pinpoint the sphere of life or personality trait that is under attack from outside circumstances. Under normal conditions, it is only the Jupiter, Saturn, Sun or Mercury mounts that become callused. If the Jupiter mount is callused, leadership qualities, generosity and sense of direction are battered and eroded by life events. If it is the Saturn mount that is callused, the awareness of progress in life, business ability and personal finances are bruised. Should the Sun mount bear a callus, sociability, aesthetic sensibility and sense of fun are challenged. A Mercury mount with a callus indicates a withdrawal into self, slow wits and difficulty with self-expression.

WHAT I HAVE A SCAR ON ONE OF MY MOUNTS?

Scarring, whether by accident or by a self-inflicted wound, is significant. Scars are usually seen as shallow, white lines, which can be easily distinguished from a natural palm line. Each scar reflects a single event that has affected the personality, and this has no bearing at all on the physical cause of the scar, whether it was caused by a slip of the bread knife or a childhood fall. The psychological scar could emanate from a tricky divorce or an emotional shock. If a scar is nearly healed its effect will be lessened. If it is fresh, vivid and red, its impact will still be current. A scar on the Mercury mount, for example, will highlight an event that has compromised the person's ability to communicate or reason.

THERE IS A MOLE ON ONE OF MY MOUNTS

A mole acts as a point of focus, concentrating the strengths of the mount on which it appears. A mole on the Venus mount signifies an increased sense of beauty and of the quality of things; and it usually relates that the passions are roused by something in particular, perhaps a person, a way of life or a favourite food. A mole on the Jupiter mount, however, speaks of a mind with its ambition and concentration focused on one goal.

WHAT ABOUT WARTS?

Traditionally it was belived that a mount blemished by a wart or warts indicated a problem associated with the qualities of that mount, which had become out of control. Someone with a wart on their Mercury mount would express themselves negatively, be over-critical of others or worry obsessively about one issue – get those warts seen to.

So many planets

It might seem confusing to know that some planets have a hand shape, a finger, a mount and a line named after them, but this makes sense if the hand is considered as a whole. The Saturn finger is joined to the Saturn mount, and the Saturn line (which some people call the fate line) usually runs into the Saturn mount.

Thumbs

When it comes to discovering how determined and strong you can be, the most important part of the hand is the thumb. This oddly shaped digit is what makes the human race special. Many mammals, even rats and squirrels, have primitive thumbs, which allow them to grasp their food, but not even the apes and monkeys have thumbs that can match ours for usefulness.

Your thumb is divided into three sections, known as phalanges. The first is the thumb's top, tip to knuckle. This signifies willpower. The second is called the 'waist,' from the top knuckle to the next, and shows intellect. The third is the boundary of the Venus mount, from the second knuckle to the joint above the wrist, and it mirrors attitudes to love and physical passion.

WHAT TYPE OF THUMB HAVE I GOT?

First, study the whole thumb, carefully assessing its size in proportion to the hand. Is it thick, thin, long or short? Relax your hand and see which way your thumb is held.

Afterwards, make a note of the answers to the following questions. If you are in doubt, compare your own thumb to the illustrations.
• Are your knuckles big or small?
• Is the first bigger than the second or the other way round?
• When you bend it back away from your hand, is your thumb supple or stiff?
• What shape is the first phalange? Is it well developed and tapering towards the nail, bending back in an arch or bulbous?
• Is the second phalange straight or bulging or has it got a noticeable waist?
• Does the third phalange bulge out from the hand?

SHORT, THICK THUMBS

The shorter, thicker and clumsier a thumb is, the more practical, sensual and materially orientated a person is and the more liable its owner to enjoy and emphasize the physical pleasures of food, sex and drink. They also respond to provocation with action, anger or aggression.

LONG, GRACEFUL THUMBS

A long, graceful thumb speaks of refinement, tact, good manners, cultural awareness and a thoughtful nature. The owner will think before acting and consider the consequences of their actions.

SMALL, WEAK THUMBS

The smaller and weaker the thumb, the more feeble-willed, non-confrontational and lacklustre is its owner. Such people shy away from confrontation and are willing to be led by others.

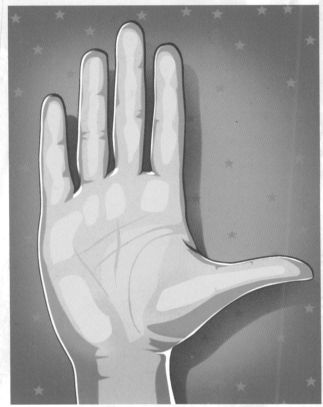
Thumb at right angle

limited means and security to forcing change and experiencing unsettling conditions.

THUMB HELD FURTHER AWAY FROM THE HAND

The further away the thumb is held from the hand, the more explosive, radical and independent the character and the more capable it is of forming opinions, making decisions and finding the gumption to enact them.

THUMB HELD AT RIGHT ANGLES TO THE HAND

If the thumb is held at right angles to the hand, it shows arrogance, immense determination to do whatever is willed and a volatile nature. If someone conceals their thumb when they talk to you they have something to hide.

THUMB HELD NEAR THE HAND

The nearer the thumb is naturally held to the hand, the more timid and introverted the character. This attitude signifies a narrow mind, which even prefers

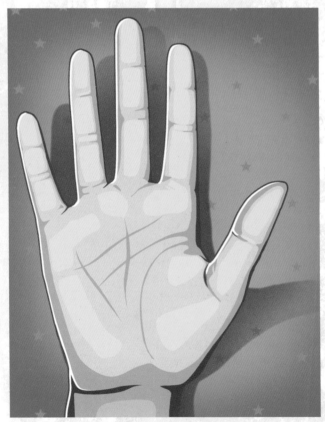
Thumb held near the hand

SUPPLE CURVING THUMB

A thumb that is supple, curves away from the hand and bends back easily, shows flexibility and openness to new ideas, a relaxed nature that is home-loving and generous with time, money and affection. These people adapt well to any circumstances or type of work and come up trumps in an emergency. They love a little adventure, the occasional social splash or far-flung journey but enjoy getting home again and back to normal life.

STIFFER THUMB

A less flexible thumb suggests iron willpower, ideas fixed in tradition (personal or cultural), perseverance, courage, loyalty, honour, patriotism and enduring friendship, love and fidelity. There is also limited ability to express feelings. Many thumbs fall between these two extremes, and there is a mix of associated qualities.

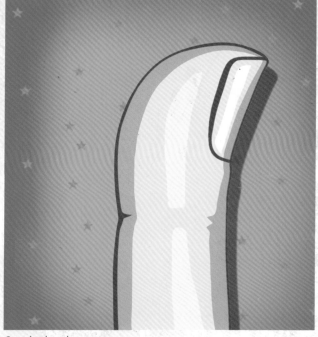

Supple thumb

WELL-DEVELOPED FIRST PHALANGE

Determination is shown by the first phalange – it should be well developed, rounded and tapering slightly to the thumb's tip. Tapering is a sign that the will is controlled and expressed in a disciplined way. A strong first phalange echoes the determination and motivation to take control of the life path. People with this formation make something of themselves and the gifts fate has given them.

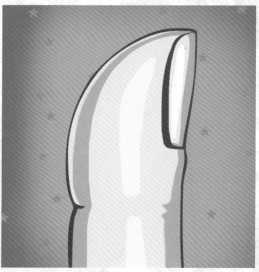

A well-developed first phalange

FIRST AND SECOND KNUCKLES

Better developed first knuckles point to powerful, logic-driven thought processes with the mind controlling the passions. A more robust second knuckle reveals strong sexual and emotional drives and the greater their need for expression. The feelings will win the day and sometimes challenge the intellect's perception of right and wrong.

Bulbous

Sloping

Extreme waist

BULBOUS FIRST PHALANGE

Should the first phalange be thick, bulbous and clubbed, the owner's willpower will be strong but uncontrollable, at the mercy of lust and anger. Such people need to develop an understanding of their own failings and find the will to change.

SLOPING FIRST PHALANGE

When the front of the first phalange slopes from the knuckle to the tip, communication skills are good and tact comes naturally, but there is less willpower and a more flexible attitude to beliefs.

SECOND PHALANGE WITH A STRONG WAISTLINE

If the second phalange has a prominent waist, the mind analyzes in depth and tries to see all sides of an argument before making a decision. Such people are attentive to detail, eloquent and capable of lateral thinking – making radical or intuitive assumptions to solve dilemmas. They excel in science, research, mathematics and literary studies.

SECOND PHALANGE WITH AN EXTREME WAIST

Extremely 'waisted' second phalanges suggest neurosis, irritability, inability to make decisions, fussiness and obsessive behaviour. Such people worry constantly about all manner of things – often a chance remark or other people's troubles – and become over-stressed. They often vocalize their concerns, whinging, whining and nagging. A large first knuckle seems to emphasize this tendency, probably because it increases caution and makes it less likely that problems will be sorted out.

FULL SECOND PHALANGE

This indicates mental processes that thrive on reason, inquiring into everything with cold logic. In extreme cases this gives a rather emotionless mentality. If the flesh tends to be hard, the person will also be blunt, set in their ways, unlikely to change opinions and often bigoted. If it is soft, they'll be open to suggestions, once they've been thought through.

BULGING SECOND PHALANGE

If the second phalange bulges out, little logic or thinking goes on. Selfish concerns, immediate needs and wants will dominate.

POWERFUL THIRD PHALANGE

Because it is closely allied to the Venus mount, the stronger the third phalange, the more powerful the sexuality and sensuality and the greater the tendency towards fickle passion, romance, fantasy and seeing life through emotionally rose-tinted glasses. This phalange is normally slightly longer than the other two, but if it is much longer, it is considered to be the ruling influence.

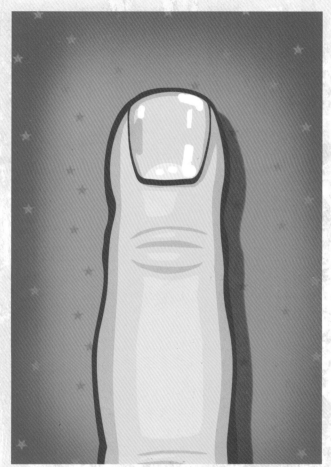

Bulging second phalange

Full second phalange

WHICH PHALANGE IS STRONGEST?

Have a look at the three phalanges in relation to each other. If all are of a size and equally strong, you have discovered a perfectly balanced individual. Most often, however, one phalange is greater. If it is the first, strength of will rules. If it is the second, reason and thought dominate. If the third, the physical drives and romantic notions are predominant.

The Palm Directory

Welcome to a new and better way of learning to read palms, pinpointing strenghs and weaknesses, and predicting the future. These chapters cover all the main areas of life and answer the most frequently asked questions about life: love, careers, children, health and more.

The small pictures on each chapter opener are simply examples of some of the many palms you'll find within the chapters. If you decide that one of them matches your own palm, then you can turn straight to the page indicated to read about yourself. However, don't worry if none of them resembles your own palm – you are certain to find one that does as you read through the chapter.

If you feel your palm has characteristics of two or more of the palms, turn to all the relevant pages and read the parts of the text that apply to you. Doing this should answer all your questions and allow you to put a picture of yourself together, like a jigsaw.

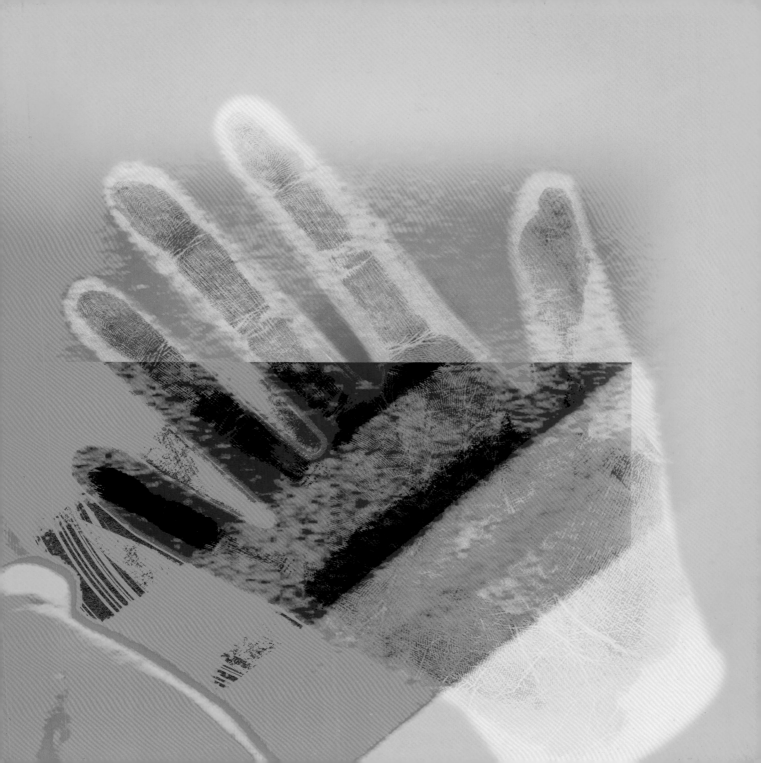

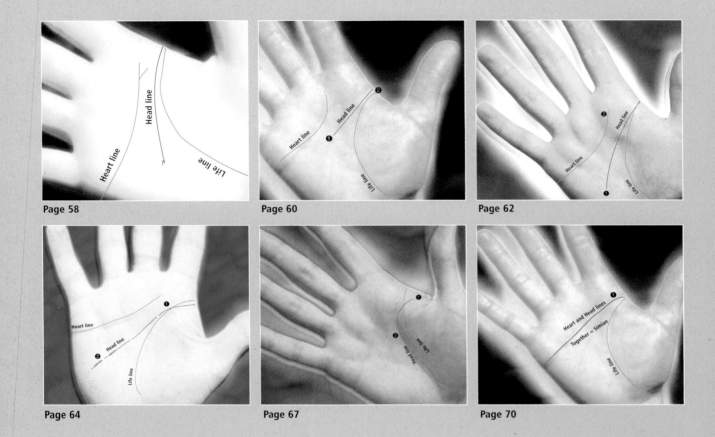

Page 58

Page 60

Page 62

Page 64

Page 67

Page 70

Everything you do revolves around how you think and how you use your mind. This chapter could answer many of your questions about how your mind functions. Are you imaginative, flexible and open to new ideas, or stuck in your ways? Would you describe yourself as determined and driven, or weak willed?

How Does My Mind Work?

4

How Does My Mind Work?

In order to answer this question we need to look at two lines, the head line, which governs the mind, and the heart line, which rules the emotions. But what is the mind? The mind is our reasoning and organizing command centre.

Our drives and passions, whether for love, revenge or reproduction, derive from our genetic programming, evolved over millennia. Other impulses, such as desire for food or sleep, are even more primeval, emanating from basic physical needs.

It is the mind that receives and organizes all this information and decides what to do with it. It also gathers finer perceptions and intuitions. It's our interface with our soul, a connection that allows this intangible being, the essential 'us', to express itself and act in the material world.

The head line is the core of the 'self,' revealing how we cope with the elemental drives and mould them to produce our individual personality, which is an expression of how we exercise our free will.

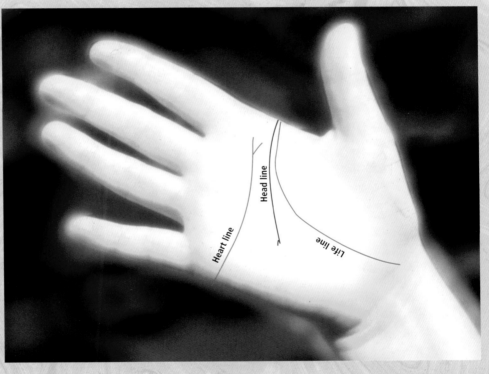

The head line's relationship with the heart line shows how much of the decision-making process is based on logic and how much on emotions. Some emotional input is necessary for any decision, but when either the heart line or the head line dominates too strongly, problems occur.

IDEAL HEAD LINE

This is perhaps the ideal head line. It starts below the Jupiter mount, a little above the life line ❶. This grants a fair amount of self-confidence – certainly enough for the owner to get on in the world and not be frightened of being seen as an individual. It reveals someone who is willing to be active and become involved in life, with quick wits but a sensible amount of caution.

The head line is strongly marked, which means that it is deep and easy to see. The stronger a head line is, the more willpower and solid determination there is to get things done. The line runs almost straight across the palm, just sloping down a little. This slope empowers the imagination and enables innovation, appreciation of the arts and the ability to be idealistic.

The heart line is just the right distance above the head line ❷, so opinions and decisions will be based on the right mix of reasoning and emotion.

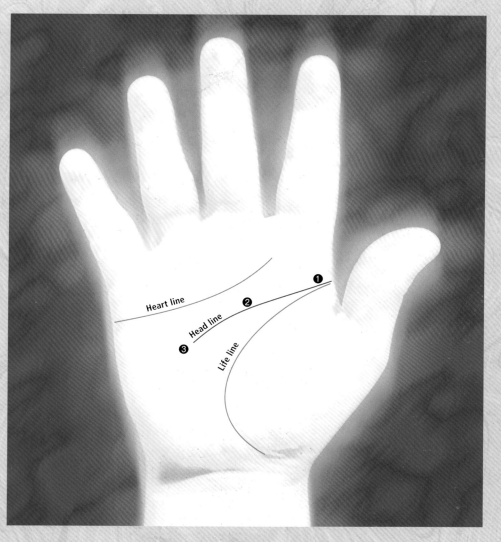

Heart line

❶

❷ Head line

❸

Life line

The head line ends below the Sun mount ❸, which would grant a clear sense of the importance of ambition, of working hard and of getting on in the world. This usually becomes apparent only in adolescence or just afterwards.

PRACTICAL

The head line on this palm is short, barely reaching the centre of the hand ❶. This speaks of a practical, pragmatic nature, with a lack of imagination and a tendency towards tunnel vision. In other words, it suggests someone who doesn't like change, who prefers to operate within set routines and who is better suited to follow rather than lead the way.

The line is also powerfully marked, which adds an element of stubbornness, indicating that anyone with this line would become truculent if challenged.

There is, however, a great capacity for concentration, which is ideal for focusing on anything practical, such as woodcarving or construction. The creative ideas and designs might have to come from someone else, but the job will definitely get done.

The head line starts barely above the life line, which points to a lack of confidence ❷. This could be shown by fake bravado, perhaps, or by getting annoyed in difficult situations.

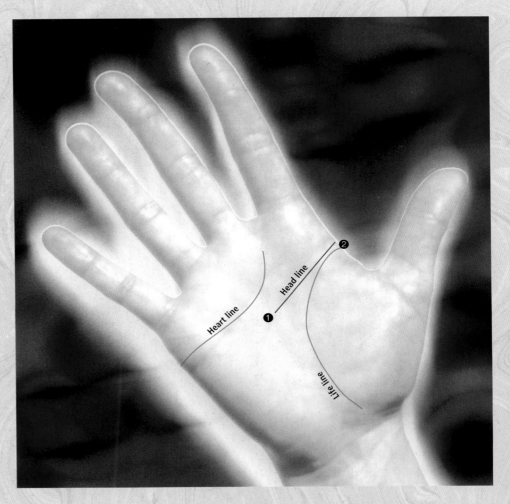

In addition, the head line is much stronger than the heart line, and there is a healthy gap between them, so the decision-making process is unlikely to be affected by emotional considerations.

LONG AND STRAIGHT

The deep head line emanates from the life line itself under the Jupiter mount. The line is straight and runs across the hand, ending below the Sun mount ❶, and it is a fair way below the heart line.

The straightness and length of this head line indicates immense strength of will and huge powers of concentration, even to the point of obsession. Once an idea is firmly in the mind, all the stops will be pulled out. There will be an aptitude for planning strategically and a love of making these schemes work.

A head line starting as part of the life line suggests a well-developed sense of caution ❷. It will take time for the owner to reach a conclusion and even longer for it to be acted on. Every single angle will have to be considered and weighed up at length.

The distance of the heart line from the head line is in indication that the emotions will be submerged, even repressed. Self-control will be a major character trait, although this could be taken

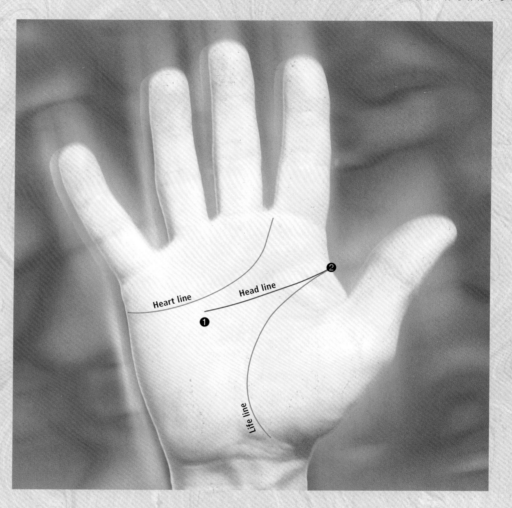

to extremes and turn into an unwillingness to take risks and so lose opportunities.

A powerful heart line shows emotional sensitivity. The feelings will be repressed but can be easily wounded, and there will be a marked dislike of criticism.

GENTLY SLOPING

Here the head line begins from the life line and slopes gently down the hand, until it reaches a place below the boundary between the Sun and Mercury mounts ❶. The head line is of average strength. The heart line, dips down towards the head line.

This hand belongs to someone who is cautious, sensitive and self-controlled and who generally knows what they like and dislike.

The length of the line grants ambition and a sense of destiny. This hand's owner will feel that they are going somewhere in the world.

As the line curves across the hand, the imagination will be alive with ideas and innovations, enjoying art, music and literature, conversation and ideas. Political and moral ideals will be embraced, and he or she will probably be a good communicator.

This hand will need a creative expression of some sort, whether it is in oil painting, gardening or poetry.

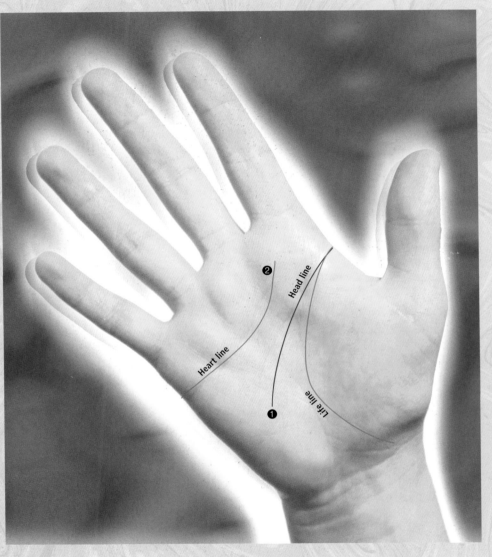

The strength of the heart line and the way it moves into the head line's territory ❷, gives the emotions sufficient energy for them be an important factor in decision-making. Passion will be fired and sustained by the vivid imagination.

UNUSUAL

This is an unusual hand. A strong head line begins slightly above the life line, and as it progresses across the palm, it curves up towards the fingers, ending its journey between the second Mars mount and the Mercury mount. ❶

The line is strong and long, suggesting not only set ambitions and goals but that there will also be the determination and focus to achieve them. The heart line is far enough away not to allow the emotions to alter any life plans. ❷

A head line that curves upwards symbolizes great success in business or finance. The mind will have an instinctive understanding of money, how to attain it and how to make it multiply. There will also be an uncanny knack for investing in the right stocks or shares, for backing the best business or invention or for starting the right venture at the most opportune time.

Combined with an insight into money is a deep comprehension of time and its power. This means that the owner of this hand will have a gift for

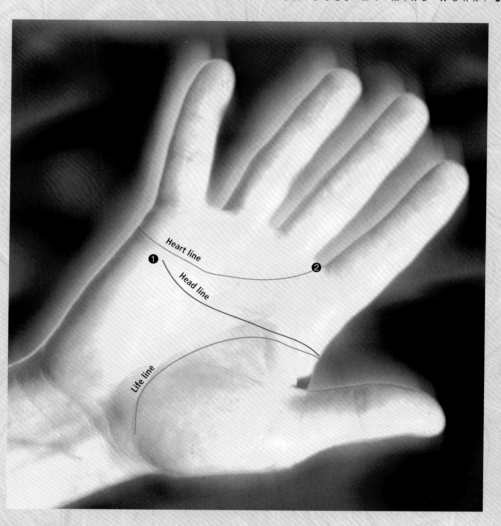

doing things at the right moment and will understand the value of patience and of allowing time to flow by. The deeper a line like this is, the more driven its owner.

If an upward-curving head line actually reaches the Mercury mount, the achievement of success and wealth will be greatly magnified.

EMERGING FROM THE LIFE LINE

This head line is born within the life line ❶, emerging from it beneath the edge of the Saturn mount and curving down across the palm. There are also a few minor breaks and some chains on the line ❷.

A head line that starts within the life line suggests a worrying nature, extreme sensitivity, highly strung nerves, shyness, a tendency to obsessive compulsions and, sometimes, an impaired constitution easily affected by periods of stress. A person with such a head line would be constantly irritable and have difficulties relating to others.

This is exaggerated by the fact that it is a long, downward-sloping head line, indicating a vivid imagination that stimulates worry and anxiety. The line's length means that concerns about the future will be a source of insecurity and stress.

Minor breaks in the line signify periods of nervous tension and of stress that is sufficient to prevent focused thought and, in extreme cases,

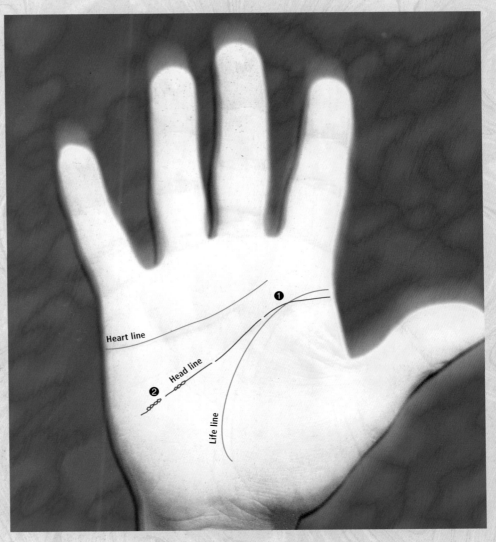

Heart line

❶

Head line

❷

Life line

even lead to a breakdown. The chains show times of indecision and lack of direction.

When the head line begins deep within the life line, behaviour is usually anti-social or misogynist, and the personality is withdrawn. If your head line is like this, make sure that you take time to relax.

BOHEMIAN

This head line begins just above the life line ❶, which indicates that the owner will have a certain amount of confidence. It slopes right down the hand onto the Moon mount, indicating a creative imagination, idealism and a mind orientated towards romance and fantasy rather than reality ❷. Such a person would be unworldly, impractical, lacking in logic and drawn to Bohemian lifestyles.

Art, music or writing could be a focus of their life, but someone with a hand such as this will rarely have the drive or practicality to become successful in any creative field. It is doubtful if much artwork would be produced, either. It is more likely that the person would drift form one art form to another.

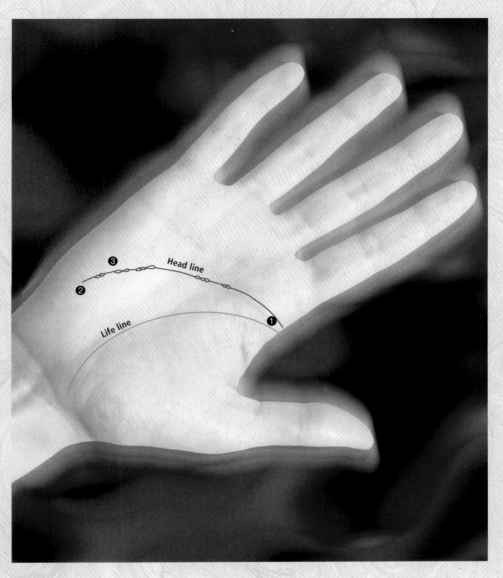

The downward-sloping line is one of the signs of an addictive personality, and it is also a mark of the 'black dog,' depression, giving rise to negative thoughts and lethargy. This is emphasized because the line is attacked by chains ❸, causing the mind to wander and adding to its indecisiveness.

ENERGETIC HAND

The head line begins up on the Jupiter mount ❶ and touches the life line ❷ before it shoots across the palm in a determined straight line. There's a light curve, indicating the owner has an imaginitive mind.

There will be natural talent that will make achievement easier. In addition, there will be energy, daring, and courage, solid reasoning powers and a firm grasp of how the world works. It is the hand of a person who would make a good leader and who is responsible and fair.

The line reaches almost into the second Mars mount ❸, a sign of huge determination. This is a person who is really going somewhere. They know what they want to achieve and will be sure to find the best way to do it.

When the head line starts on the Jupiter mount but doesn't quite touch the life line, there will be a lack of judgement when it comes to managing people and a greater tendency to take risks. This sort of mind is excellent in a crisis and in everyday life would always makes the most of opportunities, especially those that arrive by chance.

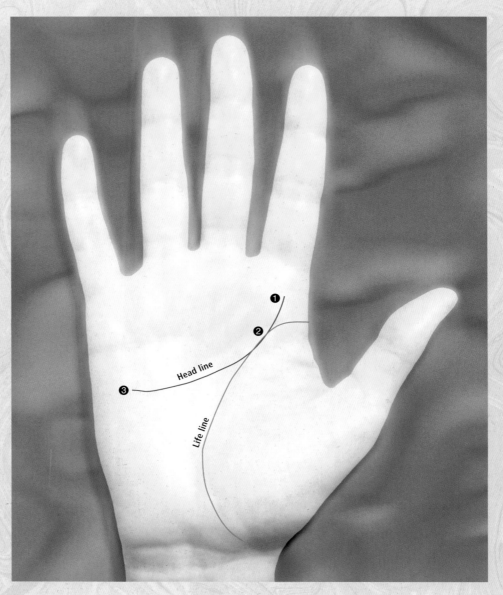

Head line

Life line

NERVOUS TROUBLES

The head line emanates from deep within the life line **❶**, a formation that promises a neurotic, worrying nature. Once the head line emerges on the other side of the life line, instead of running across the palm it follows the life line's path, hugging it closely. There are also little breaks in the head line **❷**.

Such an extremely sloping head line is not a positive omen. It robs its owner of self-confidence and self-esteem. This is a person who lacks the ability to promote themselves in any way and is unable to make decisions. They will be extremely sensitive and painfully shy. This increases the mental pressure and can lead to bouts of depression, sometimes agoraphobia or simply a dislike of mixing with other people. The breaks in the head line tell of periods when the mind's ability to function properly is impaired, either through illness or accident. In this particular case, the problems will be linked to the former cause. These breaks symbolize periods of mental illness or nervous trouble. Fortunately, normal life and the ability to cope returns, because the head line becomes whole again.

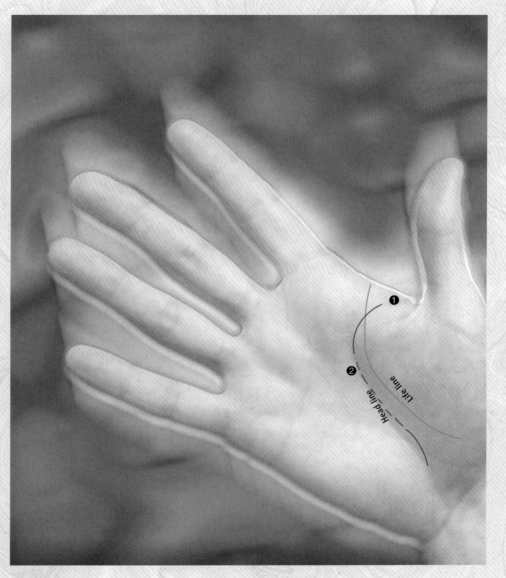

SELF CONFIDENT

The head line on this hand starts high above the life line on the Jupiter mount **❶**. It's a curving line, which slopes down the hand and terminates below the Sun finger **❷**. The heart line is low and invades the head line's territory.

The head line's high beginning boosts the person's self-confidence to such an extent that it can become a liability rather than an asset. Decisions are taken on the spur of the moment, imprudent things are said rashly, thereby running the risk of upsetting people, and impulses are listened to and acted on rather than being controlled.

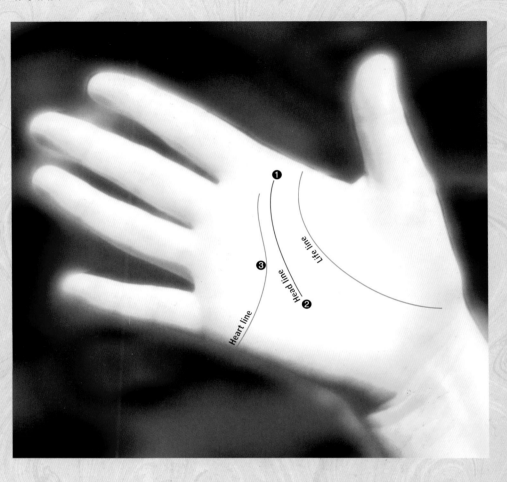

The slope of the line enhances the imagination and the appreciation of beauty and the arts.

The fact that the heart line is low down **❸**, challenging the head line's space, indicates that the emotions will dominate the intellect. The feelings, especially romantic love, will lead this personality into difficult relationships, to experience unrequited crushes or even to be involved in abusive relationships. It is a case of the passions and feelings being so strong that any

sense of reality or impartiality will be missing altogether or at least overridden.

These power-filled emotions could relate to situations other than to sexual or romantic love. They could be an attachment to a parent, friend or sibling. No matter what the relationship that stirs these feelings, happiness will depend on the quality of the person on whom they are showered: being besotted with someone is an invitation to manipulation.

TWO HEAD LINES

Don't worry if you appear to have two head lines. Such a hand actually brings a lot of benefits, adding charisma and fuelling the impact you have on the people you meet – once seen, never forgotten.

A double head line brings great intelligence, great willpower, eloquence and the ability to convince others, even to manipulate them. This power of persuasion can be turned to positive uses, especially in guiding someone who lacks direction or is experiencing personal traumas. It can also influence friends or family members to take the best direction in their lives. It also, however, brings responsibility and the difficulty of deciding who really gains from every piece of advice, the advisee or the advisor.

A person with such a hand can hold two contrary opinions about the same thing. This duality enters other spheres of life: one side of the personality could be kind and tolerant, gentle and sensitive, while the other could be hard, domineering and more ruthless.

Here, one head line starts from the life line and gently curves down the hand ❶. The other is born way above the life line and hurtles across the palm in a straight powerful line ❷. This gives the dominant tendency.

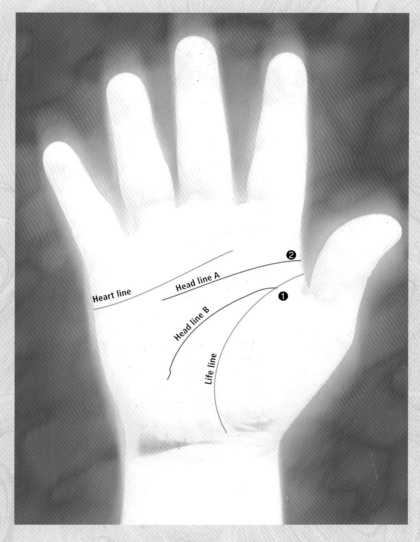

Heart line

Head line A ❷

Head line B ❶

Life line

If you have two head lines but they are not like the example shown here, find each of your head lines in the Palm Directory and read them individually. You should then choose which head line you want to be in control.

THE SIMIAN LINE

The head and heart lines on this hand are welded into a single long, strong, deep line that crosses the palm ❶. The configuration is known as the simian line, and it is a straight line, more or less in the position of a regular head line, but slightly higher. It starts quite a way above the life line.

It is called the simian line because it was once believed that people who possessed this type of line had a less evolved consciousness and were at the mercy of their instincts and desires, in the way a gorilla or chimpanzee might be. This is complete tosh.

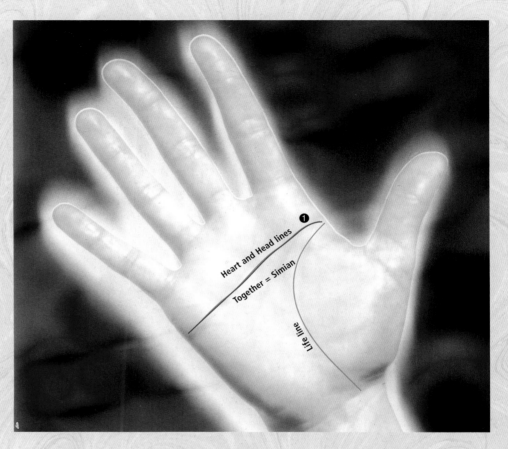

American dermatoglyphics researchers Dr Ruth Achs and Dr Rita Harper found that this line was a clue to birth defects in babies, and some midwives search for this formation as a clue to whether a baby has Down's syndrome. However, of the many thousands of hands I have studied, quite a few have possessed the simian line, and their owners are as 'normal' as the rest of us.

The simian line reveals that all the passion of the heart line is channelled into whatever purpose the intellect chooses. It shows great determination and a sense of purpose, and gives an individual a marked determination to get their own way. It grants tremendous powers of concentration and the ability to focus on realizing goals.

The simian line is found on the hands of those who have had to overcome hardship, a difficult start in life or troubled periods later, and of those who have had to find and draw on vast reserves of passion and willpower to do so. The emotions have become one with the intellect, so that the mind and heart work in unison, to overcome tests and challenges. It is the mark of a survivor.

CHALLENGED FROM BIRTH

This head line is entirely formed of tiny broken lines, islands, circles and crosses. There is no continuity in the line at all.

This palm is rare, and if you are reading this book yourself and searching for a match for your own hand, this is not it. A hand such as this represents a mind that is incapable of functioning. This is the case from birth, and it's either a genetic problem or the result of some adverse event that affects the embryo's development.

Islands and short, thin hair lines reflect physical problems with the brain that restrict its powers, while crosses are signs of misfortunes. Each circle describes a time of greater impairment or challenge. In extreme cases, the heart and life lines are similarly affected.

This sort of formation can occur elsewhere on the palm, with the same inhibiting effect. On one hand I studied, the relationship lines – the lines that speak of marriages, partnerships and the like – were made up of circles, islands and crosses.

Although living a relatively normal life, the person concerned had never shown any interest either romantically or sexually in men or women and had never had a sexual relationship. They also lacked drive in the other areas of life. Despite this, the person was perfectly happy, had warm friendships and held down a steady if unexciting job.

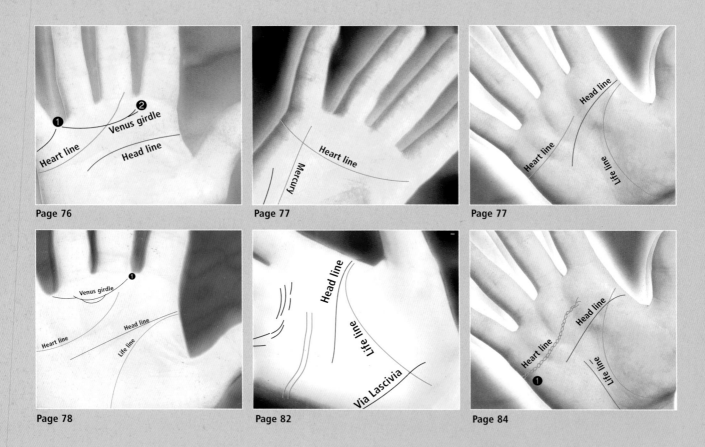

Page 76

Page 77

Page 77

Page 78

Page 82

Page 84

On these pages you'll find out whether it's love and romance that drives you, or sex and passion, and whether you seek a traditional family life, or a more easy going lifestyle with looser relationships. Most importantly, you might find a clue as to what type of loving union is going to make you happy.

Emotions, Passions and Desire:
How Do I Feel?

5

Emotions, Passions and Desire: How Do I Feel?

The hand is full of love. To judge the feelings, it is necessary to study the Venus mount, thumb, heart line, Venus girdle, family lines, head line and the via lascivia.

Love is 'a many splendoured thing', a rainbow of varying emotions, which change in intensity with our moods, age and experience. Here we explore not only romantic love, but also feelings for friends and family, physical desire and loyalty. How we love determines how we relate to the important people in our lives, and in many cases how happy we feel.

Hand shapes tell us about our attitudes to sex. People with Sun hands enjoy sex. Venus hands do if they are courted correctly. Saturn hands enjoy love-making in the right place at the right time. Mars hands can be physical. Moon hands dream about it, but are not physically driven. Mercury hands have a healthy appetite, but can be oversensitive.

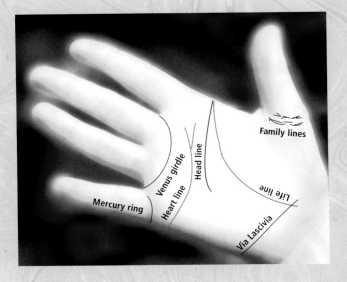

Family lines

Venus girdle
Head line
Life line
Mercury ring
Heart line
Via Lascivia

The Venus mount

• How the Venus mount is formed and how it feels are excellent guides to the strength of someone's sexual desires. A large Venus mount talks of a sensual, tactile nature and a tendency to enjoy the physical pleasures, whether it's making love, eating well or drinking fine wine. If a large mount is soft, there'll be plenty of interest in sex but libido could be lacking. The harder and more bulging the Venus mount is, the more sex is required and enjoyed. A flat Venus mount shows little interest in love-making.

The Thumb

• The thumb influences the sexual desires. The longer and stronger the thumb's first phalange, the greater the need for sexual fulfilment. A weak, short or flat first phalange hints that sexual activity won't be a priority. A person with a first phalange like this will be able to fall in love and enjoy sex, but won't want as much passion as someone with a well-developed first phalange.

PASSIONATE

The heart line on this hand is strongly marked, showing deep emotions. It begins between the Jupiter and Saturn mounts, indicating that love is balanced, loyal and passionate, homely and lasting. Friends and family will be important.

The line curves as it runs across the hand, and this brings romance and a sense of poetry into the equation. The more sweeping and curved a heart line is, the more romance and passion there is.

There is also a Venus girdle ❶, which is incomplete and formed of several lines. This indicates someone who enjoys sex. The Venus girdle makes a person sexually responsive.

Around the thumb's second knuckle there are two chained family lines ❷. This symbolizes the firm family bonds that result from a good upbringing and loving care in the family environment. The family will continue to play a role right through the life and to exert a lasting influence to the extent that the individual might do what their family wants rather than follow their own desires.

When in a relationship with a partner and children, anyone with this hand will strive to create a secure and loving family home.

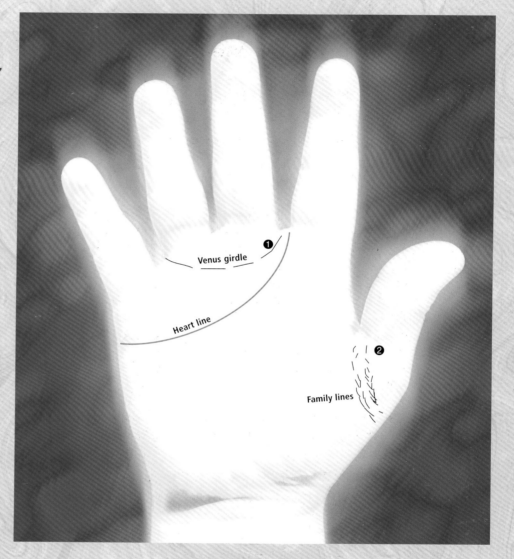

Venus girdle ❶

Heart line

❷

Family lines

AFFECTIONATE▶

This heart line is deep, basically straight but curves slightly, running most of the way across the hand, signifying a healthy sexuality and a physical way of expressing emotions.

The line begins below the Jupiter mount, indicating loyalty in all relationships, especially love bonds. A partner will be respected, their faults ignored. This person will make sacrifices for love.

If your lover or partner has this marking, they will care for you, often in a practical way.

There are two chained family lines ❶, so family ties are important, although there may have been a few problems relating to mother, father or both, but nothing out of the ordinary. These relationships will improve in adult life.

A steady life, children, a solid, loving relationship and a stable home will be the goals.

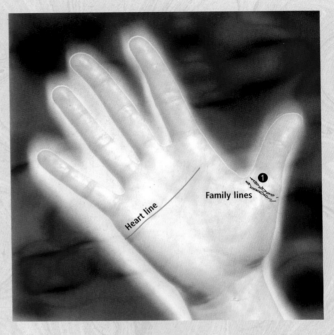

Heart line

Family lines ❶

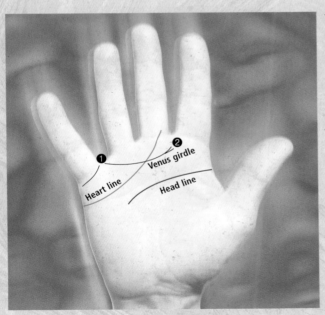

❶ Heart line   ❷ Venus girdle   Head line

◀A DARING SEXUALITY

There is a Mercury ring just below the Mercury finger ❶. This ring reveals someone who takes a strong interest in sexual matters and is unafraid of being adventurous sexually. They are restless, finding it hard to commit and tend to change partners regularly. If the Mercury ring reaches the edge of the hand, these traits are intensified.

The Mercury ring is empowered by a deep Venus girdle ❷, which confers the ability to become aroused easily.

There is no real family line, so social pressures will have little affect on this person's attitudes and behaviour. Unusually, the heart line is powerful, starting high on the Saturn finger itself. This indicates that the sex drive is high, possibly obsessive. Such a person would tend to put their own pleasure first and before that of their partner.

SLIGHTLY REPRESSED ▶

This heart line, of average strength, begins below
the Saturn mount, suggesting a person who rarely
expresses their feelings and who can be rather
cold. They tend to put practical considerations
before other's feelings and allow the daily routines
of life to dominate any relationship. Such a person
can be selfish and inconsiderate, but they can also
become dominated by a partner and take on unfair
burdens, on the 'anything for a quiet life' basis.

There is not a noticeable Venus girdle, meaning
that sexuality could be a little repressed. Such a
person would find it hard to voice their desires.

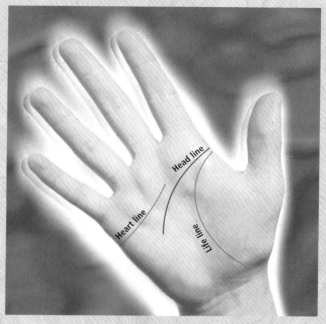

◀ OBSESSIONAL

This heart line born on the Jupiter mount gives rise
to obsessive tendencies. Any lover will put on a
pedestal and no ill believed of them. Sadly, this
person can fool themselves into thinking their lover
is exactly what they want. If and when the truth is
discovered, it results in intense feelings of betrayal
and disappointment. With the right love, however,
they flourish and are loyal, tender and caring.

The heart line is curving, which gives a romantic
nature. A well-formed via lascivia travels down the
hand, almost to the wrist. This empowers the
owner's sexuality, making passions fierce and giving
them confidence to initiate love-making.

It's easy to confuse the via lascivia with the
Mercury line: remember – the former runs from the
Moon mount while the latter begins on the Mercury
mount or just below it.

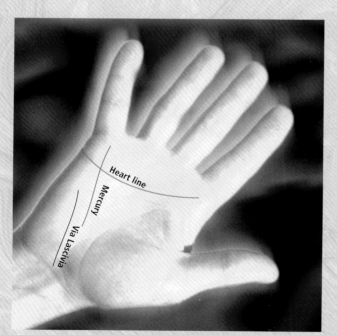

HIGHLY SEXED

The heart line of this hand radiates from the Saturn mount, a sign of a high sex drive. The line is straight, which means that physical contact and the sex act are far more important than romance or affection.

This diagnosis is supported by the presence of a Venus girdle ❶, which adds to the enjoyment of sensual pleasure, and by a via lascivia ❷, which runs from the Moon mount across the life line and into the Venus mount. This is traditionally an emblem of a person who cannot control their desires, and on the hand of someone who is neurotic, it can even point to sex addiction.

The head line is straight and powerful, suggesting that the person will exhibit strong willpower and that practical considerations will be allowed to rule over romance and, perhaps, the feelings of a lover or partner. There is a wide space between the head line and the heart line. This generally indicates liberal thinking, but on this sex-orientated hand, it could be interpreted as slack morals. The gap also signifies that public opinion will mean nothing. A person with this hand will do exactly what they want.

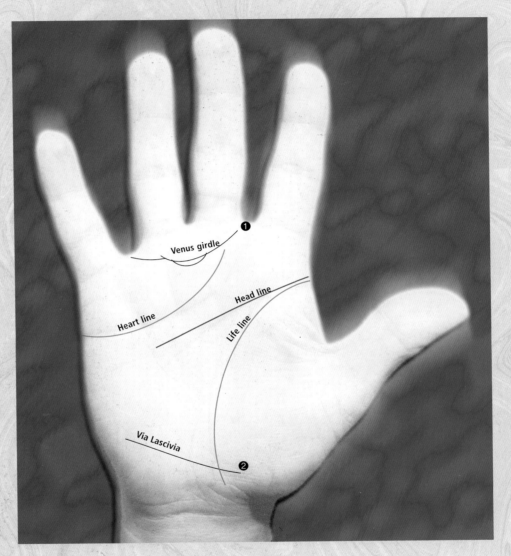

Venus girdle ❶

Head line

Heart line

Life line

Via Lascivia

❷

JEALOUS NATURE

This heart line comes down from the Jupiter finger and runs across the hand ❶. Its curling natures suggests a romantic soul, but a heart line from the Jupiter finger indicates an idealistic, overpowering, obsessive love. The lover or partner would be almost worshipped, and jealousy would be intense.

It is even possible that someone with this line could become obsessed with a stranger or a celebrity.

There is a single, straight family line ❷, an emblem of independence from the family. Love bonds with parents, brothers and sisters may be strong, and family support be available in principle. The love may be accepted and reciprocated, but the help would be refused.

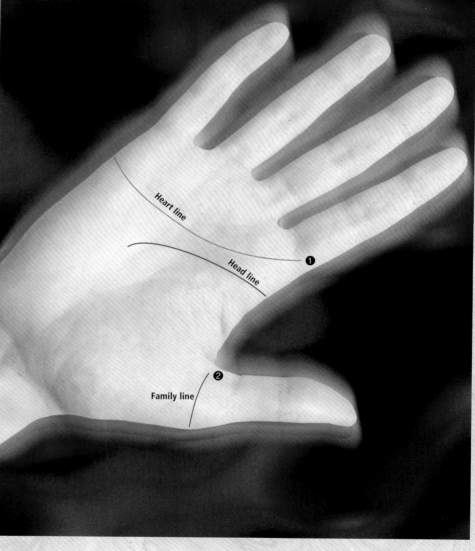

A person with this line would resist accepting aid from any relatives through pride, defiantly proclaiming, 'I'll do it on my own, my way'. They would want to forge their own way through life, doing what they want to do. It is usually a sign that there's been at least one difference of opinion with a close family member, normally a parent. No compromise would have been reached.

PURE LOVE

A heart line beginning with a fork on the Jupiter mount is said to give the purest type of love. Rather than 'pure' in the non-sexual sense, however, it indicates a real depth of emotion that will last the test of time, loyalty and concern for the feelings of others.

Sometimes a fork is wide, as if the heart line had two birth places, perhaps one on the Jupiter mount and another between Jupiter and Saturn. In such a case the emotional traits will be a mix of both.

This hand also has the beginning of a Venus girdle ❶, showing that sex will be seen as important and enjoyed as part of a loving relationship.

There are two unchained family lines ❷. A stable family life will be important and family responsibilities taken seriously. However, although someone with such a hand will like to please their parents, it's extremely unlikely that pressure from them or other relatives would have any effect once their mind was made up. Independence of thought and action would win the day.

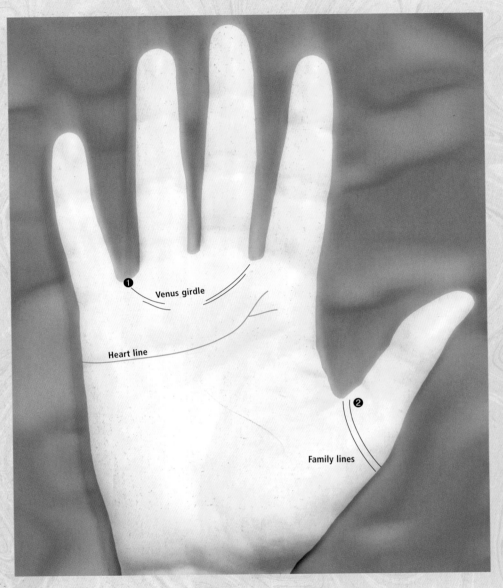

Venus girdle

Heart line

Family lines

DISAPPOINTED BY LOVE

This is quite an unusual hand. Although all the other lines can be seen, there is no real heart line, just a few remnants here and there ❶. The heart line was probably present at one time, but has faded away. It tells of a soul that has become hard and unfeeling after a deep disappointment in love. This was probably accompanied by a breakdown, which would have affected other relationships, such as those with friends and family, resulting in feelings of alienation.

If the heart line is completely absent, it is because the person is cold and unfeeling and unable to form emotional or social links.

The family lines are marked with a grille and have been reduced to a series of short broken lines and islands ❷. This reveals a less than inspiring home life during childhood and later. There would have been disruptions and emotional difficulties with one or both parents and possibly siblings, too. This would all have left deep scars on the adult mind, and the

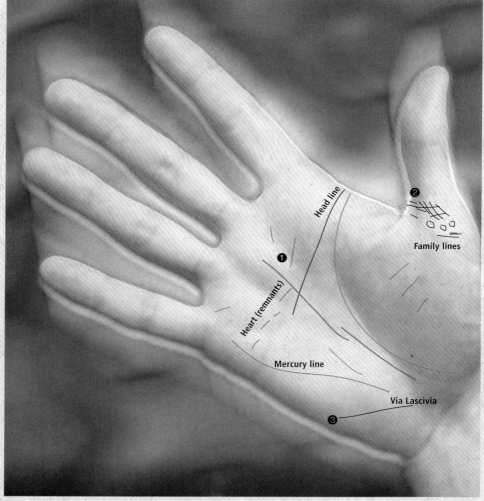

prospect of settling down into a family life would not appeal.

The hand is not without sexuality. A via lascivia runs from the Moon mount ❸, boosting the person's interest in sex and giving the necessary state of mind to find a partner and make it happen.

TWO HEART LINES ▶

Double heart lines travel close together across this palm, starting beneath the Saturn mount, a pattern that has the effect of increasing sexual energy and vigour. The start under Saturn emphasizes a focus on sex rather than on love.

There is a multiple Venus girdle ❶, which promotes sensuality. The more girdles there are, the weaker the willpower when it comes to the possibility of indulging in pleasures.

A via lascivia runs from the Moon mount to the Venus mount ❷. With this powerful sex line the owner of this hand will have difficulty in resisting the temptations of love. Fortunately, the head line is well marked and long, indicating that there is sufficient willpower to exert some self-control and adding a logical perspective.

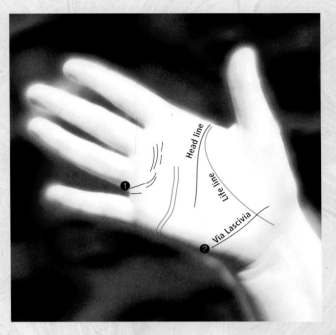

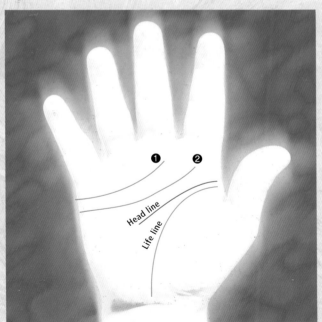

◀ CONFUSED LOYALTIES

Here a second heart line is largely independent of the first. The wide space between the two heart lines reveals an ability to love deeply – sometimes two different people at once. Unless the person has remarkable willpower and is able to avoid becoming involved in love affairs, this formation brings more than the usual difficulties linked to love and sex.

When love goes wrong, friendships and family relationships will be affected. The hand doesn't lack emotion, but its expression could bring problems.

Each heart line has to be read separately. One line begins under the Saturn mount ❶, the other under the Jupiter mount ❷. This gives emotional balance; Jupiter's influence provides a sense of idealism and romance, while Saturn's effect emphasizes the importance of sex. Those with double heart lines can't be relied on for loyalty.

PASSION AND JEALOUSY ▶

A heart line stretching right across the palm indicates an excessively loving and passionate nature ❶. The slight fork at the beginning of the line ❷ shows commitment and loyalty in a relationship and a nature that is responsive to both love and sex.

The long heart line, combined with the strongly developed Moon mount, increases the person's capacity for jealous feelings, and the creative imagination associated with such a powerful Moon mount could become a problem if they imagine that there is infidelity where there is only loyalty and blows every little indiscretion out of all proportion. The higher up the palm the heart line lies, the more passionate, possessive and jealous a person can be.

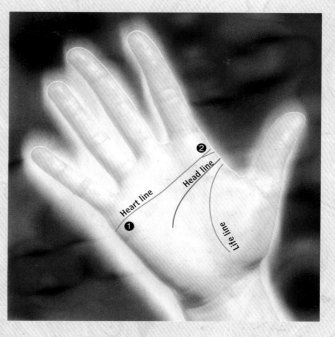

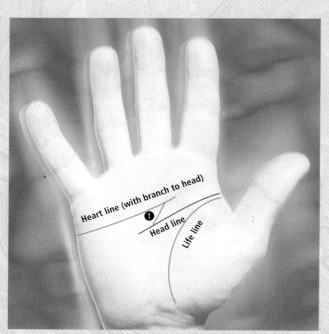

◀ SLOW TO IGNITE

The heart line here is low down on the hand, indicating a nature that is difficult to arouse emotionally and is slow to fire up sexually. Everyone has emotions, but someone with this formation would be rather insensitive and more likely to take a pragmatic view of things.

The lower a heart line is on the hand, the colder and more emotionally distant a person will seem.

A line branches from the heart line and runs to the head line ❶. It reveals a point in the life when the emotions are subjugated to the will and the head learns to rule the heart. This shift is rarely reversed.

All events on the heart line can be dated by referring to Hand 16 (see page 85).

FLIRTATIOUS ▶

The heart line is chained along its entire length ❶. The chains symbolize flirtatiousness, and someone with a heart line like this would be a constant flirt, always seeking attention and probably getting into mischief a few times because of it.

Most hands have one or two chains on their heart lines. This is normal, as many of us are or have been prone to the odd flirtation at some stage. When the segments of the chain are small, the flirtations are brief. If they are longer, the association goes on for a greater period of time.

A heart line will sometimes start with chains, and later become a single, pure line indicating someone who had craved attention, emotional and sexual, but grown out of it, either becoming more enlightened or settling into a solid relationship.

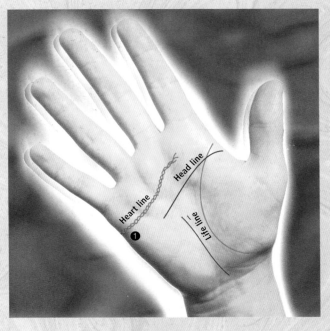

◀ ALL TAKE AND NO GIVE

The space between the head and the heart lines on this hand is narrow ❶. The smaller this gap, the less generous a person is in any relationship. The hand reveals selfishness, a narrowed outlook on life and an unwillingness to see other people's views. This person will expect a lot from their relatives, friends or partners but gives little in return.

A head line running extremely close to the heart line indicates someone who would misrepresent themselves to get their own way, especially in love. This characteristic is emphasized if the Moon mount is strong.

The heart line is also broken in many places ❷ suggesting promiscuity A kinder, and perhaps more accurate reading is that each break represents a disappointment in love or a break-up.

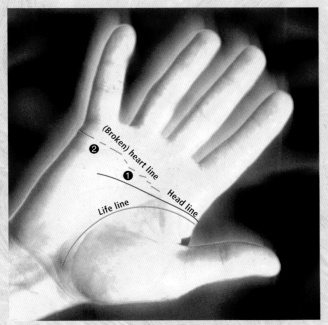

DATES

In addition to helping shine light on how we tick emotionally, the heart line records certain events in our lives, which can relate to health as well as to relationships. It is possible to read from the heart line an approximate date for any event that has an effect on that line.

If you look at the illustration you will see that the heart line is divided into three. Each section is defined by tracing an imaginary line down from the spaces between the fingers. The part of the heart line directly below the barrier between the Jupiter and Saturn fingers relates to the age 21 ❶; that between the Saturn and Sun fingers to the age 35 ❷; and that between the Sun and Mercury finger the age 49 ❸.

Not every event indicated on the heart line takes place at these precise points, so we have to assess the age when an event was experienced by mentally dividing the spaces between these points. For example, a break in the heart line below the middle of the Saturn finger would indicate an emotional upset halfway between the ages of 21 and 35 – that is, about 29.

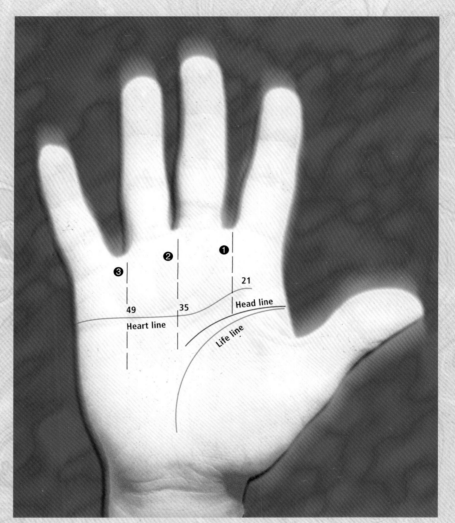

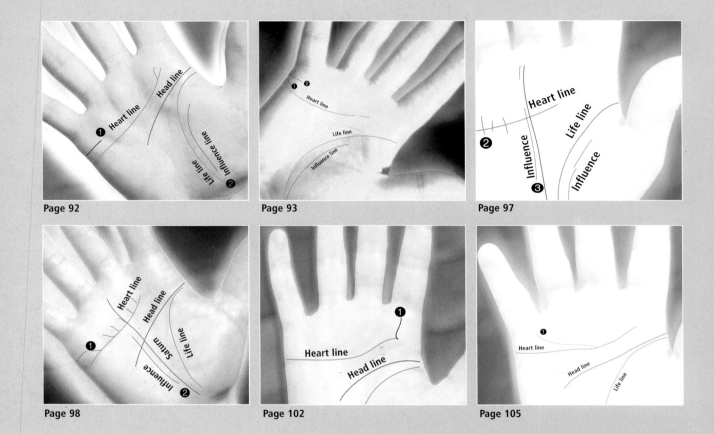

Page 92

Page 93

Page 97

Page 98

Page 102

Page 105

This is an exciting chapter, focusing on the relationships in your life, especially those that link to love and longer term unions. You may find you've got a lot to look forward to. Above are some of the palms explored in the chapter.

Love on the Palm

6

Love on the Palm

Four places on the palm must be examined to give an accurate picture of a person's love life. Most important are the influence lines on the Venus mount ❶; they follow the life line as it curves down the palm.

The relationship lines on the edge of the Mercury mount under the Mercury finger must also be studied ❷ along with the heart and Saturn lines, and any influence lines affecting the Saturn line ❸.

Remember that relationship lines relate to relationships rather than to marriages. Whether you are married or not, the relationship will be explored through the same lines. On a heterosexual's palm, a strong relationship line usually marks a marriage, but if you are gay the relationship and influence lines have exactly the same meanings.

The emotional or lifestyle impact of a relationship is displayed by the relationship and influence lines. On an extremely sensitive hand an affair of a few months will be marked as strongly as a three-year marriage on someone else's hand.

You may have to piece together the story of your own relationships from more than one thumbnail sketches.

To pinpoint the dates when relationships begin and end, see pages 85 and 89.

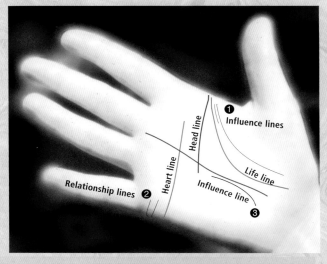

How will my love life develop?

• We are all interested in love and romance. It's natural to want to share your life with someone and a few people find one true love that lasts a lifetime. For others it is a bit more complicated. Many people have had more than one serious relationship and found that each one was 'right' for that particular stage of their lives.

• People often worry if they have more than one marriage or relationship line. There are two ways of looking at this. If you have had a major break-up in a relationship, you will be glad that there is a second bond. If you are currently with a loving partner, you can accept the knowledge that you have another relationship yet to come and, perhaps, regard this as a warning to try harder with your present partner. The knowledge could also empower you: you don't have to cling onto your current relationship if it turns stale and unhappy.

DATES ON THE PALM

Finding out when things will happen from the lines on the palm is easy once you get a little practice. Look at the illustration [right], which shows how to find the relevant ages on the Saturn line, life line and from the relationship lines on the edge of the Mercury mount.

This is an easy method because the gaps between the fingers are used as guides. After a while, you will find it natural to divide the palm in your mind, just as it is shown in the illustration. It is made easier by the marker points where the lines cross, because all are exactly seven years apart. If you are searching for a date linked to an event on the life line and it falls halfway between the ages of 35 and 42, the age in question must be 38 or 39.

The idea is to use the marker points as guides and to work out the precise age at which things occur yourself. Dates on the life line travel down the palm; while dates on the Saturn line travel up it. The space between the heart line and the

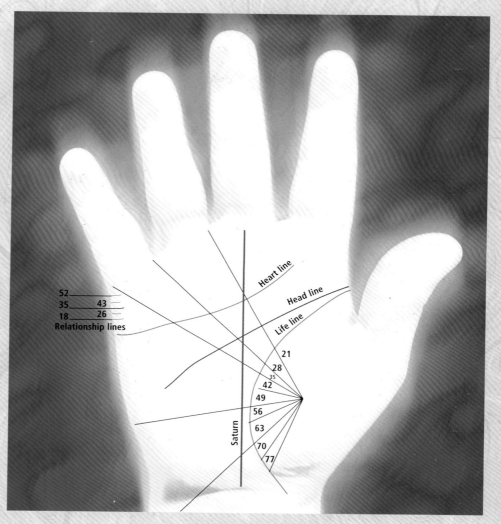

Mercury finger covers 70 or more years, and getting it right is a knack.

Turn the hand slightly so that you are looking at the side of it under the Mercury finger. Date each relationship line from its very beginning on the edge of the hand. These dates travel up the hand, in the same way as dates on the Saturn line.

FOUR RELATIONSHIPS

From the point of view of relationships, this is a busy hand. There are quite a few relationship lines on the Mercury mount, revealing at least four important relationships during the course of the lifetime and several minor loves early on.

The second strong relationship is the strongest and would probably be a marriage ❶. The fact that it is the most powerful line of the group suggests that its impact would be greater than that of the other bonds shown. Dating it from the Mercury mount indicates that it would have occurred at around the age of 35. This is also marked by a line leaving the Saturn line, which travels towards the heart line ❷. It falls short and so symbolizes a union that does not fulfil its promise and fails. This kind of relationship line is dated from the Saturn line, and the romance begins at the time the line parts company from the Saturn line.

Interestingly, there is a final relationship after the age of 57 ❸, and this is emphasized by an

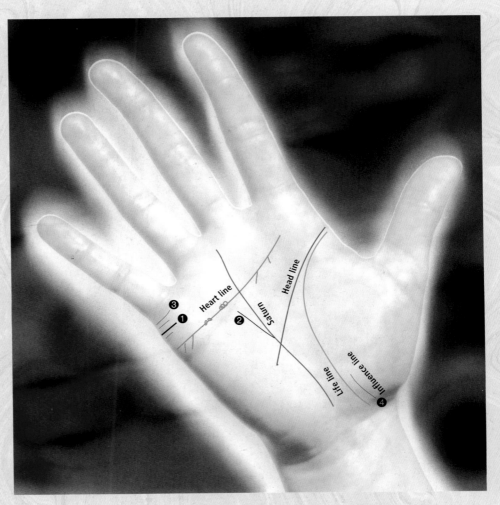

influence line that travels with the life line ❹.

This portrait of someone who has had a variable path through their love life is confirmed by the state of the heart line, which is full of islands, and there are several descending lines. Each island tells of a love affair or casual relationship, and the descending lines are upsets in love or minor disappointments.

A COMPLICATED LOVE HISTORY

It can be confusing looking for relationships on the palm, but it is usually possible with a little perseverance. Take it steadily and explore each line in turn.

This hand has three relationship lines on the Mercury mount. The middle one is likely to be a marriage rather than a liaison ❶, because it is confirmed by an influence line running by the Saturn line ❷. It occurs a little later in life – around the age of 40 – and the influence line fades out at the age of 48 or 49, as dated from the Saturn line. There is also a crossing bar cutting the heart line at this point. A bar or line crossing the heart in this way signals a disappointment in love, such as desertion by a lover or even betrayal. The Mercury line ❸ and Sun lines can be clearly seen ❹, so it is not possible that the bar could be mistaken for either of them.

The first relationship line on the Mercury mount is short and not supported by an influence

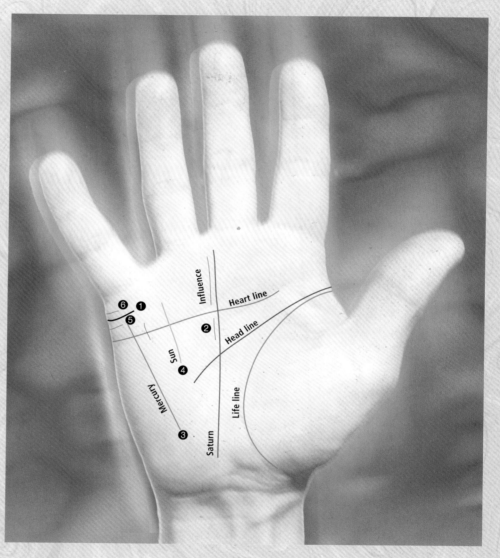

line anywhere else on the hand ❺. It was probably intense at the time but left no lasting effect.

The third relationship line is short, but it is supported by an influence line accompanying the Saturn line. It begins at around the age of 56. ❻

AN IDEAL LOVE ▶

This is a simple hand as regards love. There is one long deep relationship line, beginning at around the age of 24 ❶. The line is clear of crosses and other markings, and it has strong confirmation in a distinct influence line that runs close to the life line for most of its length ❷. On a heterosexual's hand this would almost certainly show a marriage.

The closer an influence line lies to the life line, the closer and more in harmony the partners will be.

The heart line is forked at its end on the Jupiter mount. As we saw in Chapter 5 (page 80), this signifies loyalty and a loving, thoughtful, giving nature.

This is probably the ideal hand for romance – one true love that lasts.

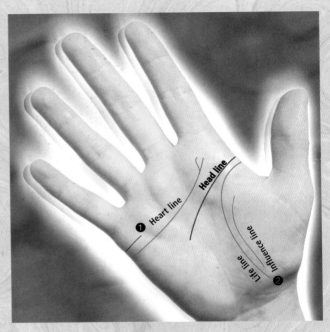

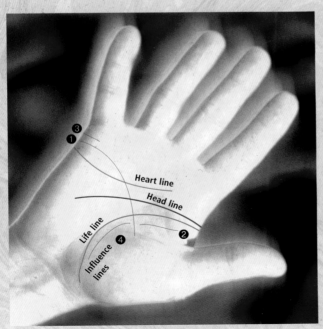

◀ A CLASSIC DIVORCE

This hand isn't quite as promising, but it does offer hope of eventual happiness.

The first relationship line on the Mercury mount ❶ is powerful and is supported by an influence line near the life line ❷. However, it runs across the hand and descends to cut the life line. The love bond would begin at the age of 19 or 20.

A relationship line that descends and cuts the life line is the classic sign of a divorce. Judge the date of the break from the point where the life line is crossed, using the life line's dating system, Here it takes place at the early age of 24 or 25.

There is, nevertheless, hope for love, because there is an equally strong relationship line on the Mercury mount ❸, also supported by an influence line near the life line ❹. This second bond would become reality at around the age of 42.

SECOND TIME LUCKY

This hand has two relationship lines marked on the Mercury mount. The first is short but deep ❶; the second is longer and stronger ❷.

The first short relationship line, which lies close to the heart line, indicates a relationship that began between the ages of 16 and 21. The line is short, not passing more than halfway across the Mercury mount, so the bond did not last. This is confirmed by the fact that there is no corresponding influence line affecting either the life line or the Saturn line at a similar age.

This relationship line is deeply marked, so it would have been love rather than a brief affair. This is the sort of line you see on the hand of someone who says: 'I did have a first love, but it wasn't meant to be.' The split is shown by a break on the heart line.

The second relationship line, the one higher on the Mercury mount, is more powerful. Dating it from the Mercury mount suggests that this relationship would have begun at around the ages of 24 to 27. If you look at the life line you will see a clear influence line emerging at the age of 25 and following the life line nearly the whole of its length ❸. This is an excellent sign, revealing a harmonious partnership. This type of line would usually relate to a marriage or a strong commitment.

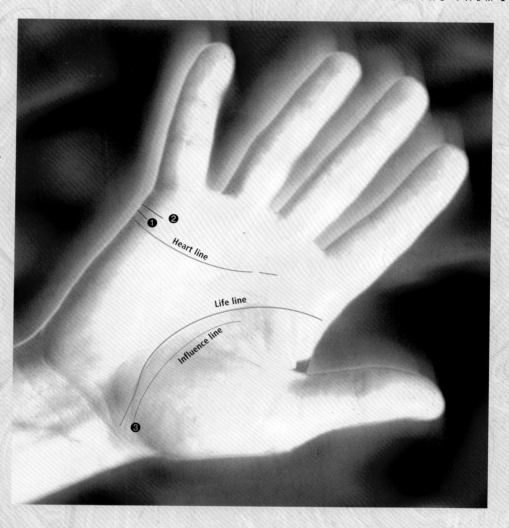

❶ ❷
Heart line

Life line

Influence line

❸

BETTER PROSPECTS

There are two equally long and powerful relationship lines running across the Mercury mount. Both have corresponding marks elsewhere on the palm, so both are marriage-type relationships.

The first bond originates at the age of 25 ❶. This is shown by an influence line on the Venus mount, which travels close to the life line ❷. There are two short breaks in this influence line, indicating temporary separations, a sign of trouble in the relationship. The line terminates at the age of 34, as marked on the life line, showing the time the marriage ended. The reason for its end is shown by the relationship line on the Mercury mount ❸. The end of the line is forked, with both branches of the fork sloping down, a sign of divorce.

The second relationship line is dated between the ages of 38 to 40 by the Mercury mount. There is confirmation that this is an important love bond on the Saturn line. An influence line leaves the

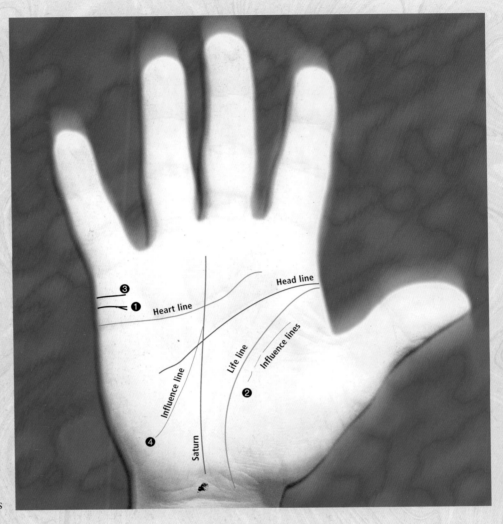

Moon mount and joins the Saturn line ❹. The beginning of the relationship is dated from the point where the line becomes one with the Saturn line. On this hand, this happened at the age of 40. An influence line merges with the Saturn line, revealing that the new partner is much wealthier and that the lifestyle is upgraded and enhanced.

PROBLEMS IN LOVE ▶

There is only one powerful relationship line on the Mercury mount ❶, supported by a significant influence line on the Venus mount within the life line ❷. This major love union starts young, at 17 or 18. The influence line veers away from the life line, indicating that, although the love bond began with great empathy, the partners will drift apart. The end of the bond is marked by the fork at the end of the relationship line on the Mercury mount.

There are tiny crosses on the relationship line, which always mark troubled spots, an event or problem that causes lasting damage. There are also a few lines descending from the heart line, emblems of disappointments and upsets in love, indicating that disagreements dogged the relationship almost from its start.

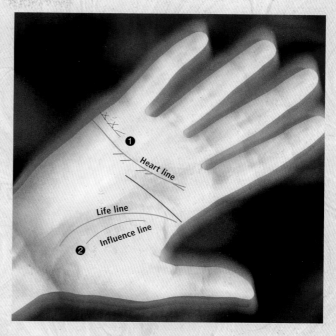

◀ AN AFFAIR OF THE HEART

This hand clearly displays two major relationships. The first relationship line on the Mercury mount is the deeper ❶, a strong love bond. There's a break in the line, pointing to a temporary separation. Further, at its end the line curves up towards the fingers, a sure sign that a relationship will end.

The second relationship line is finer and shadows the first ❷, running close to it. When two relationship lines are so near to each other, the second one (that is higher up the Mercury mount), signifies an affair. This is confirmed by the influence lines within the Venus mount. As the first influence line begins to veer away ❸, the second influence line appears and continues as a closer relationship than the first ❹, until the first disappears. The fact that the 'affair' line is longer than the relationship line shows the affair outlasts the original relationship.

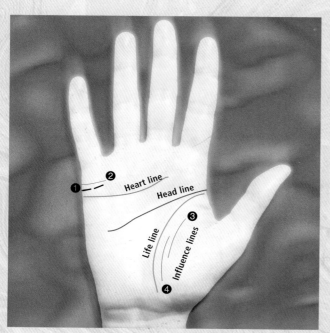

AN OBSESSION

This hand shows an emotionally intense love affair. There is a powerful first love, indicated by the first relationship line ❶ and the first influence line. ❷ The second relationship line on the Mercury mount comes into being at around the age of 33 ❸.

A third, stronger relationship line runs close to it across the Mercury mount ❹. This is a real union, but, although it is powerful, there is no real chance that it will last because the bond symbolized by the second relationship line doesn't go away. Rather, it continues and outlasts the third. This is easier to see on the Venus mount. Inside the life line all three relationships are shown as influence lines: the first, short union; the second longer relationship ❺; and the third relationship ❻, which comes into being after the second has started, co-exists with it for a while and then ends.

The power of this second love is echoed elsewhere on the palm. A line leaves the head line and runs to the heart line ❼, showing a powerful attraction, an obsession or even a destructively passionate relationship. When this event is dated from the place the line merges with the heart line (see Chapter 5, page 85), it corresponds with the second relationship, giving an age of around 33.

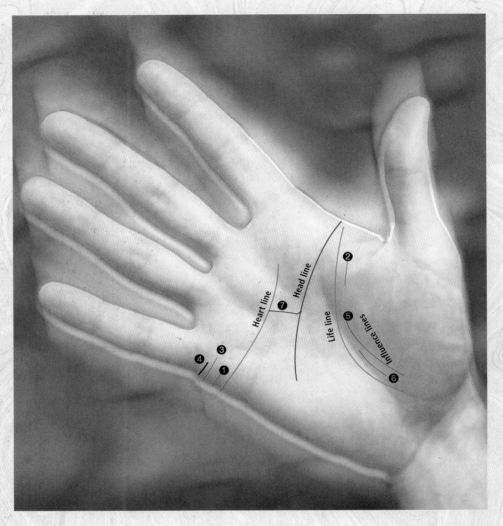

EMOTIONS NEGATED ▶

There's a single relationship line on the Mercury mount, but with two islands on it ❶. An island on a relationship line indicates a time of hostility towards the partner and usually a separation. This line also ends in an island, showing that a second separation will end in a final and permanent break-up. Islands always bring upset.

This traumatic relationship is mirrored on the heart line. A firm line leaves the heart line and runs to the head line ❷, revealing a time when the emotions are subjugated to the will – the head rules the heart. This is the point when some people 'switch off' their emotions and never relate in an intimate, loving way again. They may be quite happy with their friends and family but rarely enter into a new partnership.

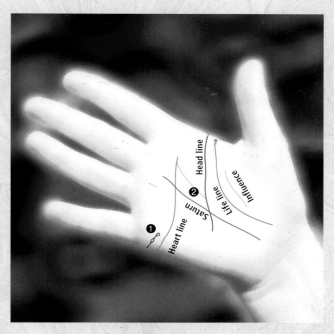

◀A WOBBLY RELATIONSHIP

The first relationship line on the Mercury mount is wavy ❶, which suggests an uneasy, unsettled and changeable love partnership. Such a line definitely does not appear on the hand of a conventionally married person with 2.4 children. Some lines show a period of 'wobble', indicating that although there was a time of troubles, the relationship endured. The bars that cut the heart line ❷ are markers of disappointments in love, let-downs and infidelities.

There is, in addition, an influence line travelling parallel to the Saturn line ❸. It actually crosses the heart line, showing a union that will bring misfortune, perhaps a loss of money or status or even simply an inharmonious existence.

Fortunately, there is a second relationship starting around age 40, shown both on the Mercury mount ❹ and the Venus mount within the life line ❺.

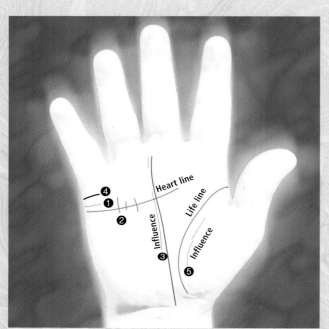

GOOD OMENS ▶

This hand is full of good love omens. There is only one relationship line on the Mercury mount ❶, supported by an influence line running close to the Saturn line ❷. An influence line running this close to the Saturn line, is a sure sign of a loving and harmonious relationship. Dating it from the Saturn line indicates that it begins at the age of 25.

The fine lines ascending from the heart line show joys and successes in love. These are not necessarily lots of excellent relationships; they may simply be good, happy times.

The relationship line on the Mercury mount bends downwards at its end. This is usually a sign that the palm's owner will outlive their partner. This can be taken negatively, but it doesn't always mean that the relationship will be cut short by death.

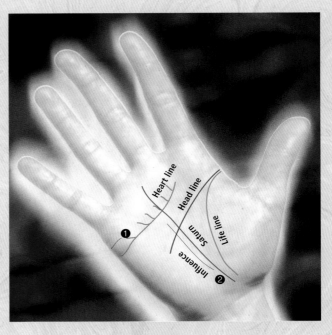

◀BAD RELATIONSHIPS

Lines emerging from the heart line and running into the life line are signs of disappointments in love and emotional distress. They can be dated from the life line. Here, the first upset is at age 36 ❶; the second at around 49 ❷.

The three relationship lines on the Mercury mount are mirrored by influence lines within the life line. The first relationship line has an island, a sign of difficulty or even separation ❸. The second has descending lines from it, indicating that physical or mental health concerns made the relationship especially challenging ❹.

Fortunately, the third relationship line is long, smooth and deep, showing a happier union ❺.

The three relationships can be dated: the first at age 19, the second at age 39, and the third at around 53.

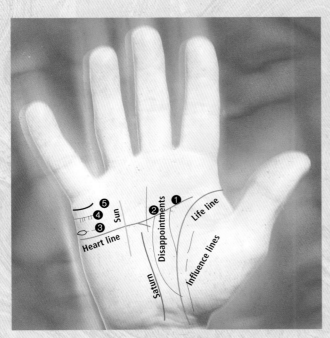

INTERFERENCE

On this hand a single firm, loving union is revealed by a relationship line on the Mercury mount ❶. An influence line associated with the same relationship runs close to the life line on the Venus mount. This love bond begins at around the age of 30.

There are three deep lines descending from the Mercury finger and crossing the relationship line ❷. These are interference lines, symbolizing negative pressure on the relationship from a close family member, friend or, in rare cases, employer. The motive in all cases would be to weaken, jeopardize or destroy the union. Fortunately, in this case the bond goes on and the attempts to disrupt it are unsuccessful. However, there are some descending lines flowing from the heart line ❸, showing times of upset and tribulation, so the pressure exerted by the malign third party did succeed and cause some dispute, upset or problem between the partners.

It's not uncommon to find these interference lines, and sometimes they do coincide with the end of a relationship. It might seem amazing that at the end of the 21st-century parents still take it on themselves to disapprove of a child's love-

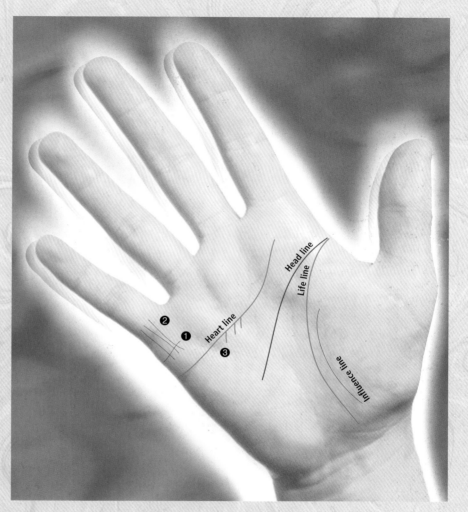

match, but they do, often with the best intentions, always causing everyone involved, including themselves, pain.

It is important to know the difference between interference lines and child lines. Interference lines come from the Mercury finger and cross a relationship line; child lines come from below the Mercury finger and stop at the relationship line.

SACRIFICES FOR LOVE

On this hand the relationship line is extended and crosses the palm like a second heart line ❶. The longer a relationship line is, the more sacrifices are made for the relationship it represents and the more the old life is left behind and the partner's world entered.

This is an extreme case, where the owner of the hand has devoted themselves to their partner absolutely and merged themselves with their ethos, to live for them, support them and be there for them. This hand shows that the arrangement has worked.

An example of this type of relationship would be a person who marries someone from another country and goes to live abroad, assuming the partner's culture and language. It might also apply to someone who marries a wealthier partner and adopts their lifestyle, leaving their own family and friends behind. Depending on the personalities involved, this can be a good thing. If, however, the dominant partner is manipulative or otherwise abusive it is not. A more positive example would be a politician's wife, who travels with her husband, raises funds for the party and makes life easy for him, allowing him to do his job. The devoted partner, depending on the hand, could be the power behind the throne.

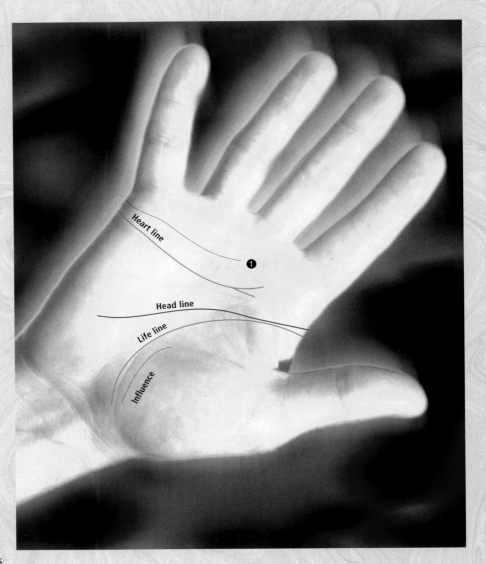

Heart line

❶

Head line

Life line

Influence

ALL'S WELL THAT ENDS WELL

This hand looks complicated. The first relationship line on the Mercury mount, starting at the age of 27 or 28, has a branch from it that runs down the palm to cut the Sun line ❶. This shows that the partner is of a lower social standing or income level. Obviously, this does not have to be a problem, but on this hand, the influence line associated with this partnership runs straight up the Moon mount ❷, before crossing the palm and joining the Saturn line. When an influence line does this, it signifies that the whole relationship is based on illusion rather than on real emotions and commitment. Perhaps the person is in love with the idea of love or, in an extreme case the relationship exists only in the mind.

An interference line also leaves the life line and joins the Saturn line, just above where the influence line joins it ❸. This speaks of active interference by outside parties, usually parents. If there is an interference line and the influence line stops short of the Saturn line, the relationship is successfully sabotaged and falls apart. Here, the influence line reaches the Saturn line, but the relationship ends anyway – there is a fork at the end of the relationship line.

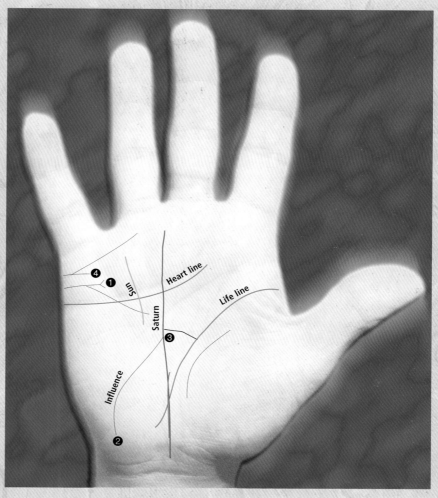

Fortunately for the owner of this hand, there is a second relationship line, beginning at the age of 36 ❹. This is a well-omened match. A deep branch leaves the relationship line and runs to the Sun mount, promising that this second partner is successful and well known. Quite the opposite of the first one.

A PARTNER'S ILL HEALTH▶

The relationship line on the Mercury mount shows difficulties ❶ The cross just above it indicates a challenge to the partner's health through accident or illness.

There are also some fine lines running from the relationship line towards the heart line, and these are signs of stresses on the love bond caused by the partner's ill-health ❷. There is also a break in the relationship line, marking a period of separation. This could be caused by a stay in hospital or a period of convalescence abroad. The relationship line starts again, so there is a reunion. There is no recurrence of the unfortunate marks, so the course of the lover's health – and the relationship itself – runs more smoothly as time progresses.

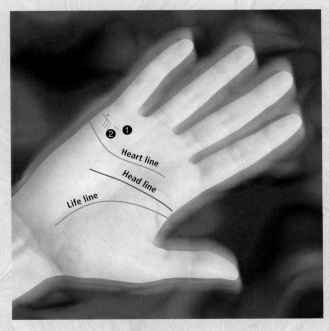

Heart line
Head line
Life line

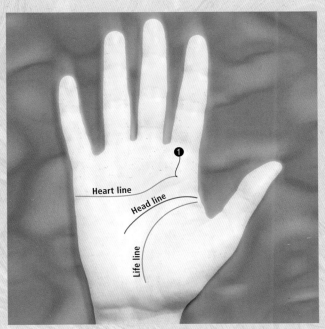

Heart line
Head line
Life line

◀DRAWN TO SUCCESS

When studying a palm you can tell which personality types someone is attracted to. This is done by looking out for lines branching away from the heart line and running to the mounts of Jupiter, Saturn, Sun or Mercury. If the branch line ends on the Mercury mount, Mercury personalities will hold a fascination; if it ends on the Saturn mount, it will be Saturn personalities.

Here, the heart line sends a branch to the Jupiter mount ❶, showing its owner is attracted to Jupiter personalites when it comes to romance.

Jupiter people are ambitious go-getters, who enjoy responsibility and are usually highly successful in their chosen field. They possess power, leadership qualities and status. Their faults can include being overgenerous, proud, ostentatious and self-indulgent.

LOOKING FOR STABILITY

On this hand a line leaves the heart line and travels to the Saturn mount ❶. This gives clues that, when it comes to love and romance, the owner of this palm will be attracted to Saturn personalities.

Saturn people tend to be reliable, patient, nurturing, wise, thoughtful, philosophical, sober and thrifty. They take life seriously and like to plan ahead. On a more negative note, they can be penny-pinching, narrow in outlook, obsessive and controlling. Most people find a Saturn partner needs a little help to let their hair down.

Careers that interest Saturn people revolve around engineering, mining, farming, teaching, accountancy or banking, architecture, research, history, property development, conservation, the utilization of natural resources, classical music or religion.

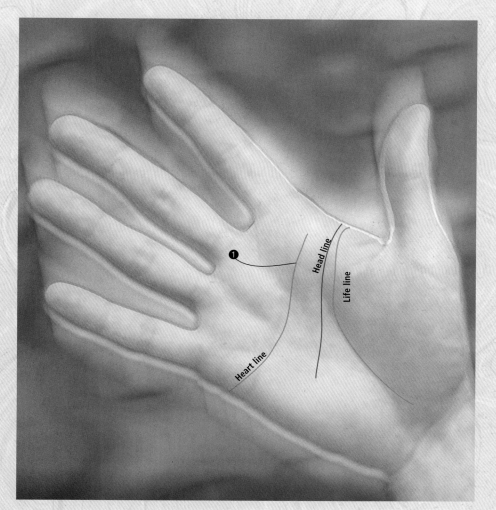

SEARCHING FOR A STAR

This hand has a branch that leaves the heart line and heads for the Sun mount ❶. This is a sign that the owner of this palm will be drawn to Sun personalities when it comes to seeking a perfect love and life partner.

Sun people are highly charismatic, laughter-loving socializers, who enjoy being entertained and experiencing the bright lights. They are talented, elegant, fashionable, innovative, imaginative, creative and often artistic. They have the gift of the gab and usually know how to use their varied gifts to make money and get ahead in the world.

Some Sun people are truly talented artistically, whether with brush, pen, piano, or in the theatre. Such people tend to be intensely charismatic and loveable. They attract followers but are not practical and usually need looking after.

Careers for Sun people will found in the field of arts or crafts, in construction, commerce, financial services, the car trade, sport, the retail sector or agriculture.

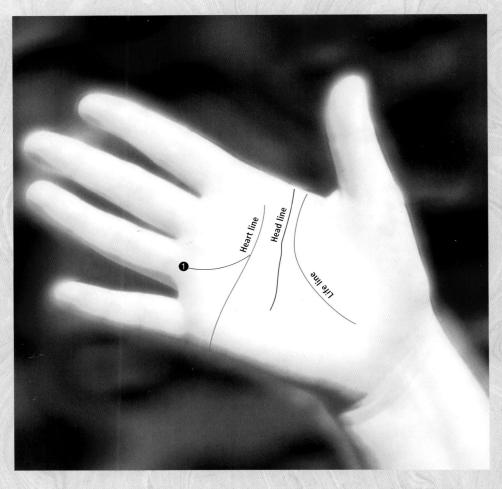

DIPLOMATIC LOVER WANTED

On this hand a branch veers away from the heart line and runs on to the Mercury mount **❶**. This is a sign that Mercury personalities will have the greatest impact on the owner of the hand when it comes to love and will exert the most powerful attraction.

Mercury people are quick-witted. They are excellent and eloquent communicators and have good bargaining skills. They are extremely flexible and can be master diplomats, but they have a tendency to do things quickly and to live on their nerves. Faults include impatience, talking and worrying too much, non-commitment and jumping from one thing to another.

Career choices for Mercury people include information technology, selling, the media, travel, education, science, medicine, psychology, marketing, the law, writing and, sometimes, politics.

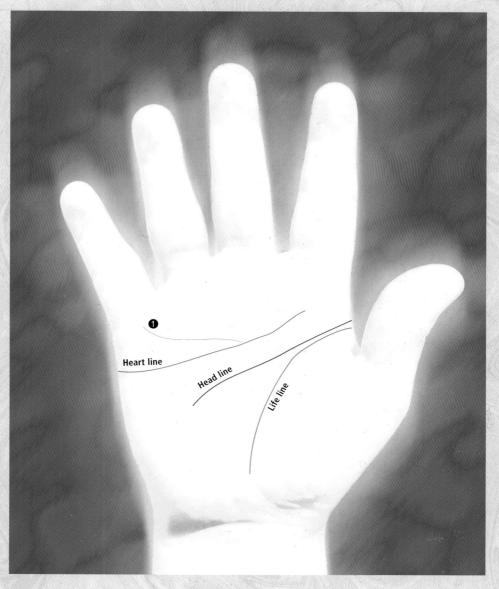

Heart line

Head line

Life line

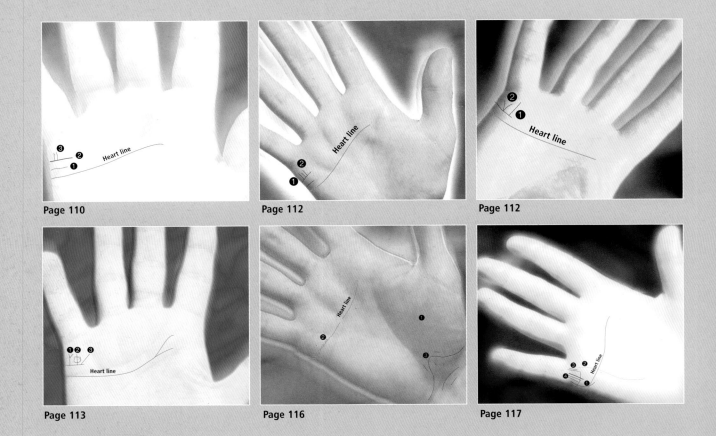

Page 110   Page 112   Page 112

Page 113   Page 116   Page 117

It's a common question, and with the help of the lines on your palm, you might get some useful answers. There's an element of choice as well, but added knowledge could help you make an informed decision about starting a family, or even explain the past.

How Many Children Will I Have?

7

How Many Children Will I Have?

Almost everybody – male, female, gay, straight, broody, for or against the idea of having children – asks how many children they will have.

This question causes difficulty for anyone reading palms, as the number of children shown on a hand is only the maximum number that could be produced. They might never actually happen. This is because, as human beings, we have free will and a fertile person can usually control the number of children they have. Some people choose not to have any at all or there might never be a 'right' time. Contraception also grants the power to decide.

With experience it is possible to judge the number of children. Bear in mind that if you are still fertile and have only one child, while your hand shows two, it's not that the palm is wrong,

it's just that you'll have another at a later date.

Strange things happen, too. For example, some hands have two children marked, when there are actually three children. In every case the 'missing' child has grown apart from the parent and lives their own life, sometimes in another country, although it doesn't necessarily mean that there's no love between parent and child.

To seek children, study the lines on the Mercury mount. The child lines emerge from the relationship lines. Other areas associated with children and fertility are the heart line, the Venus mount, the first bracelet and the Neptune plain.

Use your intuition

• Once you have been reading hands for a while you might discover that you seem to know what a hand says without finding the lines to back you up. This is your sixth or psychic sense guiding you and telling you what you need to know about the hand you are reading. When you find this is happening, accept it and let your intuition be your guide. You might be surprised at how uncannily accurate you can be.

• There is no need to worry if you find that you don't develop this gift. You can continue to read palms with excellent results.

A passion for children

• The wish to reproduce is a result of evolution. When even the most convinced anti-children men and women reach a certain age, their biological clocks turn on and they begin to feel the urge to reproduce.

• It's natural but it's not fate. It is a mechanism similar to the ageing process. Some young people experience this need so strongly that they have children, regardless of their circumstances and they may regret it later. If they had waited, the feelings would have subsided. The art is to let them have sway when material circumstances, finances and relationships are stable.

A FERTILE HAND

This is a well-developed hand, warm to the touch and with a pinkish flesh tone. The Venus mount is well developed, and the heart line is long and strong. It is particularly important that this is so towards the edge of the hand under the Mercury mount.

The hand's warmth and emphasis on the Venus mount and heart line indicate a passionate, loving nature, with a healthy sex drive.

The Neptune mount is full, and the first bracelet is in its proper place ❶, running along the border between the bottom of the palm and the wrist. These signs reassure that fertility is not compromised by problems with the reproductive system.

There is one powerful relationship line ❷, and deep marks for four children emerge from it ❸. On some hands of this kind, many more fine child lines are shown. Depending on the strengths of the child lines, this is a sign of a nurturing nature and indicates that children and family life will be a priority and a preoccupation, a labour of love rather than a necessity. If the person with this hand had been born in an earlier era, they could well have gone on to produce eight or more children.

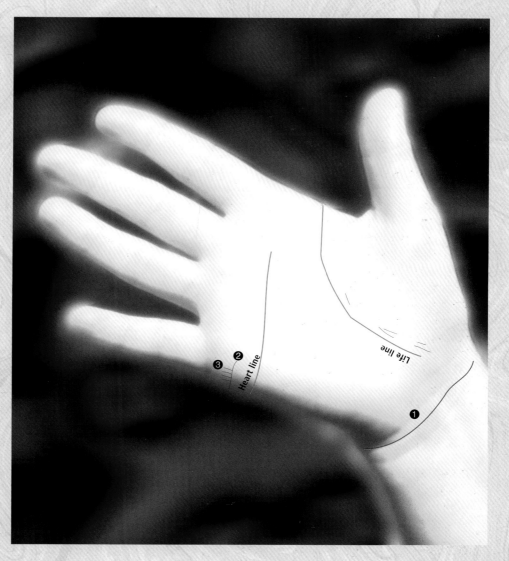

Heart line

Life line

A LOVING FAMILY

The Venus mount is of average size, and the hand itself is quite firm and warm to the touch. The heart line is strong and curving, pointing to a passionate nature. This type of palm speaks of a normal, loving nature and an average desire to produce children.

There are two relationship lines on the Mercury mount. The lower one, which signifies the first major love bond, is weaker than the one above it ❶. The top relationship line, which is deep enough to display a strong union ❷, has two child lines emerging from it ❸. This suggests that the children are the result of that union. However, even if the children are born within the first relationship, if they are raised in the second relationship and come to love their step-parent as a true parent, they will be shown as the children of the second relationship. This is complicated, but it proves that love is stronger than blood.

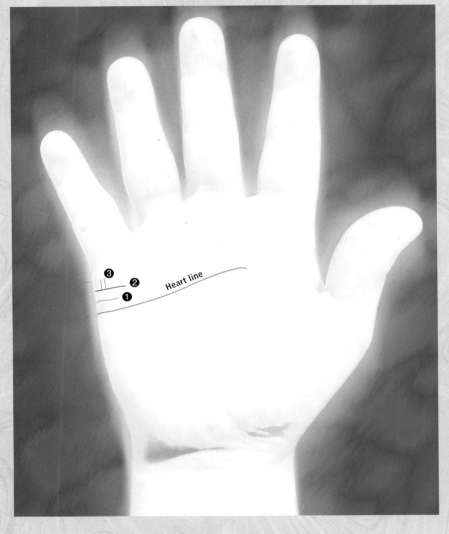

The two child lines are of equal strength, a sign that both children are of the same sex. They are fairly deep lines, which suggests they are both boys. A weaker child line would indicate a girl. It can be difficult to judge whether two identical child lines are weak or strong, because they cannot be compared. In general, it is possible to judge their strength by comparing them to the relationship line they emerge from. If the child line is weaker, it indicates a girl; if it is as strong or stronger, it indicates a boy.

A COMPLICATED FAMILY ▼

The first relationship line is insignificant ❶. The second has a powerful child line attached to it ❷. This is a son, and the extra depth of the line suggests an close bond between child and parent.

The third relationship line has three finer lines, slightly wavy, coming from the end of it nearer the Sun mount ❸. Two of these are weaker than the third.

The strong son from the second relationship would be a biological child of the hand's owner. The three weaker, slightly wavy lines, are stepchildren introduced by the third love partner – a boy and two girls. They are shown on the palm, which signifies that they have been accepted into the home and heart as the hand-owner's children but not in such an intense, tare usually absent from the palm altogether.

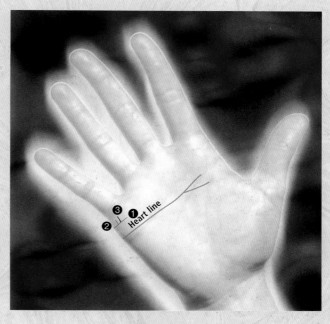

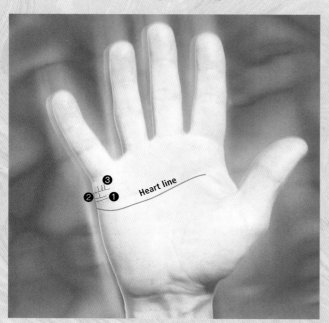

A BOY AND A GIRL ▲

This hand bears one relationship line ❶, with two child lines. One of these lines is weaker and represents a girl ❷. The stronger of the two lines represents a boy ❸.

Traditionally, the child nearer the edge of the palm is the first born, while the child who is furthest away is born last. Here, this shows that the daughter was born first and the son second.

The child lines are close together, suggesting that they were born between one and four years apart. The further the child lines are apart, the greater the number of years between births.

You can tell if the child lines show children that have already been born or if they are revealing the potential number of children. Generally, children that are yet to be born have fainter, less well-defined lines than those who have already been born.

THE PRODIGAL SON ▶

Of the three child lines that connect to the top relationship line, two indicate girls ❶ and one a boy ❷. The two female child lines are similar in length, while the one for the son is noticeably longer. This line's extra length is a clue that the son will be the favourite – a child who is doted on and smothered with affection and praise.

Although it is usually said that a parent must have no favourites, many find they have a special bond with one particular child. This doesn't mean that the others are treated any differently or given less love; it's just the natural rapport of one soul with another. A favourite child who isn't spoiled will have a line only a little longer than those of their brothers and sisters.

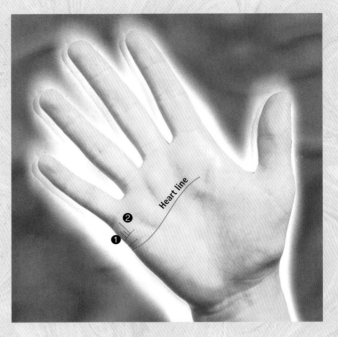

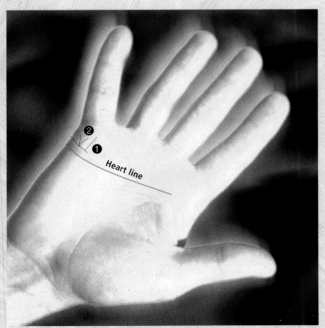

◀ TWINS IN THE FAMILY

There are two child lines shown on this hand, but between them they predict the birth of three children. The normal-looking child line indicates a son ❶; the V-shaped child line reveals the presence of twins ❷. It is a finer line, suggesting that these would be twin daughters.

The twin mark can be the upside down, showing that there will be only one child, who will inherit the gene for twins from one or both of their parents.

When twins are not identical, these marks are not necessarily shown, and the presence of the twins is indicated by two normal child lines, which may be a little closer together than usual. Biologically, identical twins come from the division of one cell into two; non-identical twins are from two separately fertilized eggs.

VARIATIONS

It is rare, but not impossible, that three child lines like the ones illustrated here would appear on one hand.

The first child line starts normally and ends in a fork ❶, a formation that is linked to twins. It signifies that although the child it represents is not a twin, they have inherited the gene for twins from one or both parents and will possibly have twin children themselves.

The second child line has a square on it ❷. Squares are symbols of protection, and show that the child has passed safely through a period of life-threatening danger, resulting perhaps from illness or an accident. If the child line is broken within the square, the threat was extremely severe, but everything turned out well in the end. The nearer the square is to the relationship line from which the child line emerges, the nearer to birth the dangerous event occurred.

The third child line is at an angle rather than straight ❸. It symbolizes a child whose relationship with their parents will be challenged, and the loving bond will be stretched, damaged and, in some cases, broken. There will be an emotional distance between parent and child, sometimes through childhood or teenage rebellion, sometimes

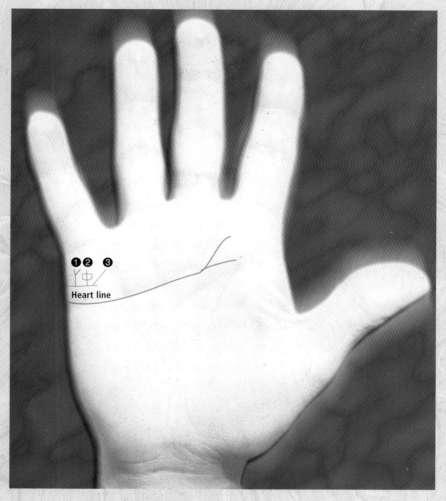

through parenting problems. This child will be unorthodox in thought and action, and the behaviour will be visible to the outside world if the line slopes towards the heart line from the direction of the Mercury mount. If the line slopes towards the heart line from the direction of the Saturn and Sun mounts, the child's behaviour will have greater impact on the family.

TROUBLES

There are four child lines on this palm. The island at the start of the first child line is an indicator of health problems for that child at the time of their birth ❶. If the island is further along the line, the ill-health will come in later life.

A small, weak child line, such as the second one here ❷, or one like the third ❸, which is made up of dashes, squiggles, islands, a cross or crosses, warns of miscarriage. Many women, probably more than one in three, experience one or more miscarriages at varying stages of pregnancy. It is perfectly normal, and most women will go on to deliver healthy intelligent babies.

The fourth child line on this palm is delicate and wavy ❹, with a few small breaks in it. This is a signifier of a child who has had health problems from the start; the child has a weak constitution and has suffered from various ailments.

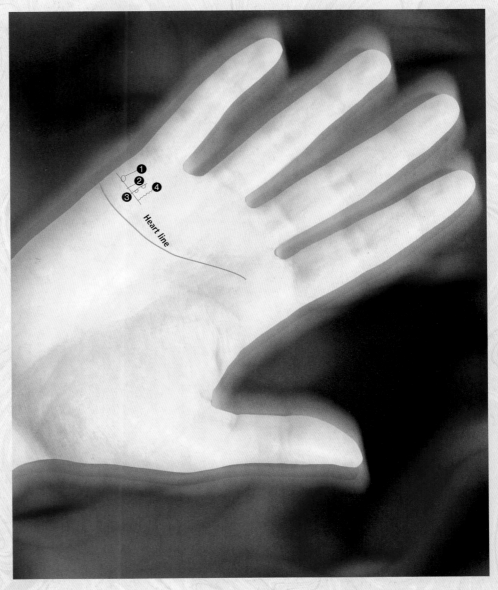

Sometimes, the line gets stronger as it travels up the hand, which tells of a return to health.

LITTLE INTEREST

On this hand the Venus mount is weakly developed ❶, suggesting little interest in sex. Of course, a lack of physical passion does not rule out a normal level of fertility or the desire for children, but it is a sign that there is no great focus on making love and reproduction. A hand like this would rarely produce more than two children.

The heart line is weak, too, especially below the Mercury mount ❷, further diminishing the need to express love physically. This can also point to physical troubles that would present obstacles to conception. These markings are not an indication of infertilty, but they suggest that it may take longer for the owner of the hand to become pregnant or that medical intervention might be needed.

One child is shown near the edge of the Mercury mount. ❸ There is a chained section on this line, warning of a period of illness. The line gets strong again, so this phase will pass.

Anyone with a hand like this would benefit from allowing themselves to be more expressive emotionally, and if children do arrive they should concentrate on displaying affection and love.

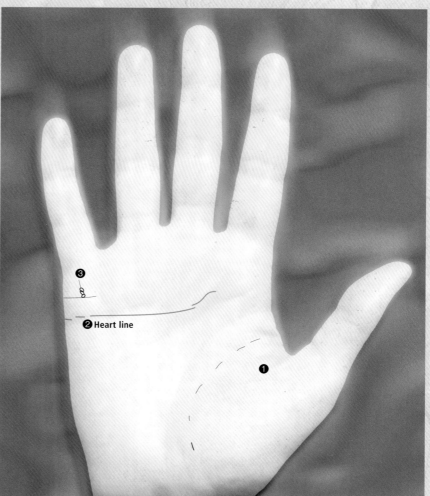

❷ Heart line

HELP NEEDED

The Venus mount on this hand is underdeveloped and soft to the touch – a sign of weak libido ❶. The heart line is faint and fragmented into islands and small breaks under the Mercury mount ❷. This warns of possible difficulties with the hormonal or reproductive systems, which will be create problems when it comes to conceiving a child.

Adding to these difficulties, the first bracelet arches up on to the Neptune plain ❸, another indication of troubles with internal organs, particularly any linked to the reproductive system. Anyone with this formation should seek professional advice if they feel they have problems with anything that links to the reproductive system.

Even if your hand displays these marks, do not give up hope of having children. Try harder and seek medical aid early on if you do not become pregnant as quickly as you hoped.

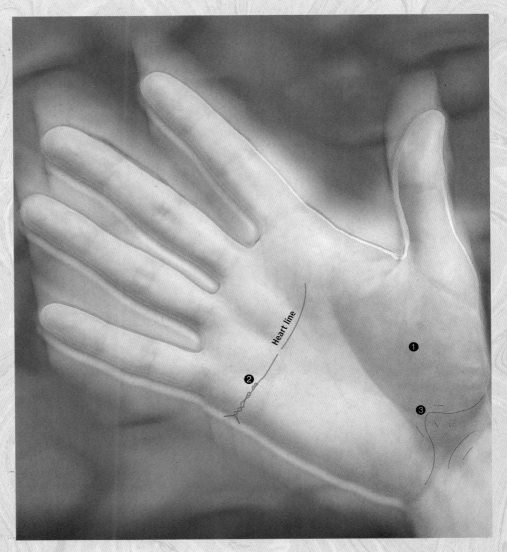

Heart line

CONFUSING LINES

This hand is shown only to avoid confusion. It illustrates the medley of other lines that can appear on the Mercury mount and be confused with child lines.

The only real child line on this hand is the one that runs through the relationship line and down into the heart line ❶. It points to a child who is spoilt and who evolves awkward and unfortunate personality traits because of it.

The Mercury line is well away from the relationship lines ❷, but it can be nearer when it can cause difficulties.

The two deep lines on the Mercury mount, lying towards the Sun mount, emphasize the powers of the Mercury mount; they are nothing to do with children ❸.

A number of powerful lines descend from just below the Mercury finger and cut through the relationship lines ❹. These are interference lines, and they indicate that there has been interference in the relationship, usually by family members or friends.

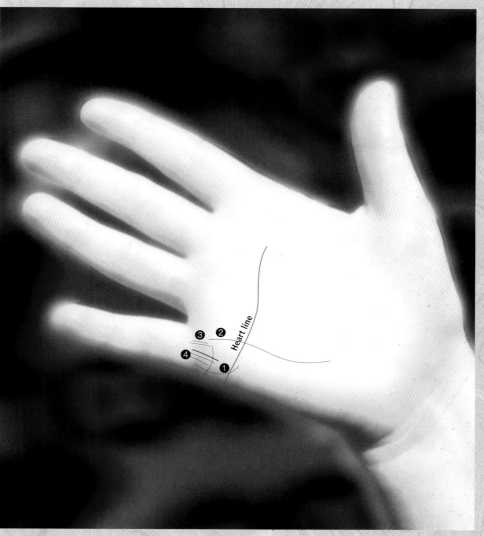

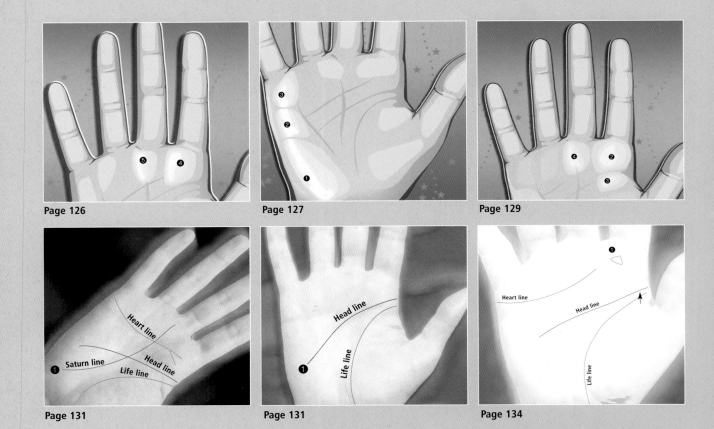

Page 126

Page 127

Page 129

Page 131

Page 131

Page 134

Every one of us has a talent or a natural instinct for a certain type of work or profession, but sometimes it remains hidden. Palmistry can unlock the door to the right career for you. If you're in a career you love, it's easier to find success.

What Sort of Career is Best for Me?

8

What Sort of Career is Best for Me?

Choosing the right career is essential for wealth and happiness. When you work in a field you are passionate about, you put in more effort, your enthusiasm is infectious, and you achieve more. If you make the wrong choice, however, you will find it hard to do your best, and disillusionment will soon set in.

Most of us leave school with a few dreams and hazy ideas, and our careers choices tend to be made for us through a combination of chance and opportunism. Palmistry allows you to work out what profession you were born to enter and whether you are likely to do best within the corporate structure of a company or would be happier if you were self-employed.

If you are settled in a working environment that satisfies you, but you nevertheless feel that you need something extra, this chapter could point you in the right direction to fill the void. You might discover that you have abilities that

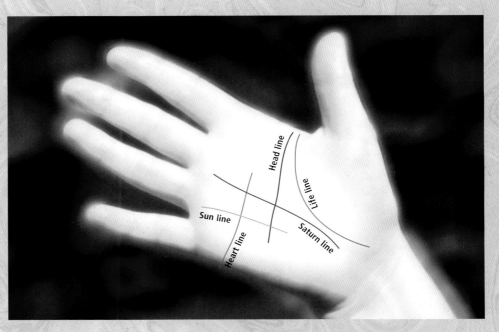

will lead you to a satisfying hobby, a creative passion or a part-time business.

Some people are blessed with what's known as a 'vocation,' an in-born leaning for a particular

Hand shapes

In Chapter 1 we looked at the seven hand shapes. These give clues about which types of career would provide useful opportunities. If you have not yet sorted out which hand shape you are, go back to pages 14–26 and find out.

Remember, if your hand is a combination of two shapes, you will have aptitudes for the types of work linked to both, which gives you more flexibility. For easy reference:

• **Sun hands:** practical occupations such as the construction industry, agriculture and crafts; financial services; the retail sector or buying and selling; the arts or professions or businesses connected to them; anything needing fast decisions.

• **Mercury hands:** advertising, marketing and sales; business; travel; the media; human resources; education.

• **First type of Mars hands:** military; travel or transport; diving; sports; agriculture; construction, engineering or demolition; the rescue services; anything that needs quick thinking and courage.

• **Second type of Mars hands:** science, medicine or design technology; education; health; politics; social work.

• **Venus hands:** work with people and communications, personnel or recruitment; advertising; telephone sales; the retail sector; food; drama; beauty, hair, fashion or massage; humanitarian agencies.

• **Saturn hands:** the arts; education; religion; military services; health; translation; the law; gardening and conservation; politics; mining and metals; archaeology and history.

• **Moon hands:** religion; education; psychology, psychiatry or counselling; politics; the leisure industry; the arts; secretary or personal assistant; administration; community work.

• **Jupiter hands:** the leisure industry or travel; maintenance; sales; any type of work requiring a wide range of skills.

career and the certain knowledge that it is what they want to do. People with vocations often find careers in medicine, nursing, the priesthood, architecture, teaching and the arts – music, literature or drama – and even accountancy and dentistry can be vocational choices. A few individuals wake up to a vocational calling later in their lives. Although they may have worked for a degree or established a successful business, they get out of bed one morning with a sudden passion to do something completely different.

Not everyone has the luck to find a career path they love, but everyone has gifts and aptitudes for certain tasks. It may be that animals respond to your touch, that people listen to you or that parenting comes easily. No matter what skill it is,

it can in some way, with a little imagination, be turned into a profession or business. If there is a vocation within you, palmistry can point you towards it.

Remember, it is never too late to make radical changes in your life. No matter what your age and training, you can find and follow your ambitions or true vocation. There is no such thing as 'I can't'. The reasons you come up with are simply excuses. We are all free spirits and can pursue our dreams. We all have responsibilities, of course, but where there's a will there's a way.

To find your career path on your palm, you need to study the mounts, the fingers, the Saturn line, the Sun line, the head line, the life line and the quarters.

What career do my fingers point towards?

The size and shape of your fingers reflect the natural talents and aptitudes that you are capable of expressing and using to get on in the world. To explore their secrets, the first step is to decide if your fingers are smooth or if they have big knuckles.

If you have smooth fingers you will do best in the sphere of inspirational work, where quick wits, immediate responses and intuitive decision-making are favoured. Look for employment where you will be dealing with people and in areas that require imagination.

If you have big knuckles you should consider work that needs thought and strategic planning. Careers that require logic, such as computing or accounting, or anything that involves craftsmanship, plumbing, woodcarving and the like or a philosophical mind, are also suitable.

If your fingers are short (your Saturn finger is shorter than your palm) you would be best working within a corporate structure, possibly in a manual role, or in anything where your involvement is direct. However, any intricate manual work would take a long time to master. You will be a better all-rounder if you can learn to be patient.

If your fingers are long (your Saturn finger is longer than your palm) you will have an aptitude for working with people and will enjoy tasks that need precision, planning and patience. You may need to practice stress control if you are in a demanding role.

People whose finger length and palm length are in balance are usually good with people, and they do well in roles that involve communications or in practical, creative or behind-the-scenes, back-up jobs.

Look at your fingertips are use the following summary to see which careers are likely to be most appropriate for you:

• **VENUS FINGERTIPS.** You could slot into a creative career, from interior designer to set designer or hairdresser. A more practical application of this would be stonemasonry or pottery. Venus fingertips are useful around an office and can make good personal assistants or human resource workers.

• **SATURN FINGERTIPS.** You would excel in a career that involves careful planning and patience. Business and commerce would be suitable, but only if you are unlikely to have to make a lot of instant decisions. In creative fields, people with big Saturn fingertips make the best jewellers and watchmakers and even composers. Fine and

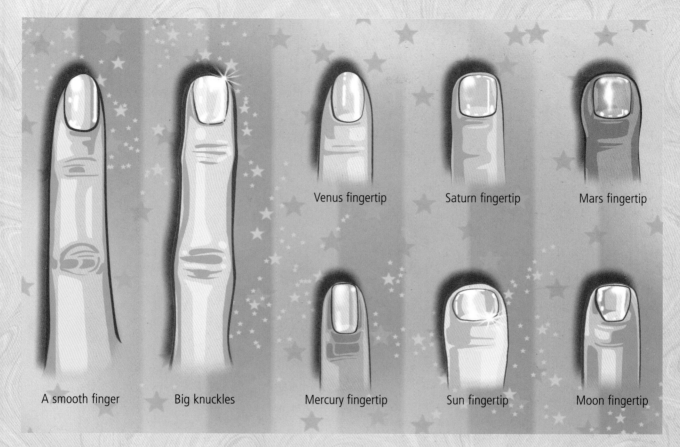

Venus fingertip   Saturn fingertip   Mars fingertip

A smooth finger   Big knuckles   Mercury fingertip   Sun fingertip   Moon fingertip

delicate craftsmanship is a forte, as is police work, particularly in a forensic role.

• **MARS FINGERTIPS.** The areas of medicine and psychological healing will attract you, as will any exciting, unpredictable work that gets you out and about. Think about a uniform if discipline is not a problem.

• **MERCURY FINGERTIPS.** You will do best in work with business, office or sales links. A communication-based role or anything that involves spreading information is likely to attract you.

• **SUN FINGERTIPS.** A career in selling or in the retail sector is likely to appeal to you, but Sun fingertips are also found on people performing manual work, often in mechanics or the construction industry. A love of life and activity will mean that transport and travel would also be ideal areas to work in.

• **MOON FINGERTIPS.** You need focus, and a corporate structure would keep your great creativity and talents rooted in reality. Moon imagination can be turned to anything, but too much responsibility would cause anxiety.

MOUNTS AND CAREERS

The next step is to determine which mounts dominate your palm. This is easy when one mount is noticeably more developed than the others, but in most hands two or even three mounts are strongest. If you have two strong mounts, the career fields linked to each of them will be open to you, but try to work out which paths would make the most of the abilities associated with both mounts.

• **JUPITER MOUNT.** Look for a career in management; the law; business; the leisure industry; politics; community-based work; the officer ranks in the services; architecture, property development or real estate; banking or accountancy; education; and sometimes art and music.

• **SATURN MOUNT.** Opportunities for a career revolve around engineering or tool making; mining; farming; teaching; accountancy and all other financial spheres; architecture or property development; research; history; conservation and the use of natural resources; medicine or psychology; the arts, especially music and writing; and religion.

• **SUN MOUNT.** You should look for a career in the media, arts or entertainment, particularly the theatre, television or film; public relations; crafts; construction; commerce; the financial services; the car trade; sport; the retail sector; agriculture; travel and leisure; and catering.

• **MERCURY MOUNT.** The most promising areas are information technology or telecommunications; sales, marketing or product branding; writing, the media or publishing; public relations; travel; education; science, medicine or psychology; the law; speech making; and, sometimes, politics.

• **FIRST MARS MOUNT.** Look for a career in the military; sports; travel or exploration; catering; metalwork, engineering or mechanics; sculpture; weapons technology; computers; psychiatry, psychology or counselling; construction; transport; research; printing; and law enforcement.

• **SECOND MARS MOUNT.** The most suitable careers involve social work or housing; history; law enforcement, the judiciary or the law; politics; religion; trade unionism; planning; conservation; the probation or prison services; the civil service; human rights activism; and printing.

• **VENUS MOUNT.** Career options include hands-on healing arts, such as massage; childcare; the retail sector; perfumery, fashion, beauty or hairdressing; floristry; the arts world; events organization; breeding animals or birds; gardening; antique dealing or restoration work; handicrafts, painting and decorating, dressmaking or tailoring, soft furnishing and interior design.

• **MOON MOUNT.** Look for a career in education; social work, nursing, surgery, psychology or counselling; photography or film-making; music; writing; travel; the navy or shipping; diving; bee keeping; catering, running a bar, brewing or distilling; the pharmaceuticals industry; and fish farming.

Halves and quarters

• One of the earliest traditions of hand reading involved dividing the palm into halves and then into quarters.

• Imagine a line running from the tip of your Saturn finger, right down the hand to your wrist. The half-hand that includes the thumb is known as the outer area; the other half, which includes the Mercury finger, is the inner area.

• The inner area expresses thoughts and emotions, while the outer area reflects activities and goals. Of course, the perfect hand has both halves in balance.

• The hand is further divided into quarters. The first quarter rules practical things and skills; the second governs ideas, science, technical talents and the intellect; the third is concerned with spirituality; and the fourth is associated with creativity and compassion.

• Most often, two quarters will dominate rather than one, and if this is the case on your hand, the tendencies of both are combined within you.

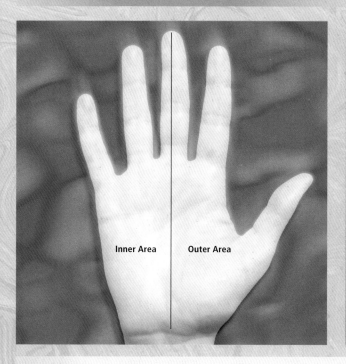

Inner Area Outer Area

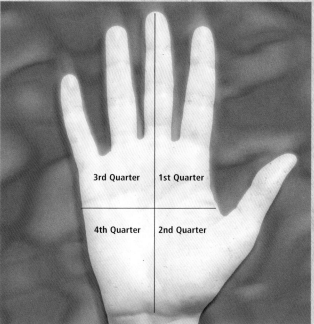

3rd Quarter 1st Quarter

4th Quarter 2nd Quarter

Making the most of the palm directory

In this chapter you will definitely discover that your hand relates to more than one of the palms shown. If you combine career information from all the hands that show parts identical to yours, you will emerge with a full picture of your capabilities.

SELF BELIEF

The outer area dominates this palm. The thumb is bold and determined ❶, and the Venus mount is powerful and well developed ❷. The first Mars mount matches it ❸, and the Jupiter mount is robust ❹. The Saturn mount is just a little less defined than the Jupiter mount ❺.

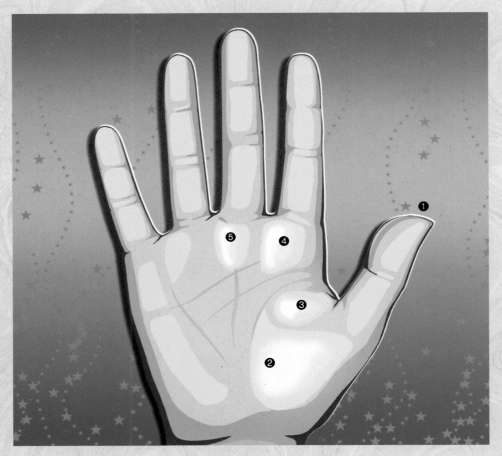

Someone with a hand on which the outer area has dominance will have a vibrant mind and will be alive to possibilities and willing to try anything once. This will be an ambitious person, with a sense of destiny and a belief that real things need to be achieved in the real world to sustain fulfilment and usefulness in life.

The areas of the hand do not point to specific career fields, but it is possible to outline the challenges that are required to stimulate the mind. A hand with a dominant outer area suggests a career that revolves around activity and challenge. If a job is sedentary and involves sitting in an office or at a computer terminal, there must be opportunities for the imagination and intellect to be given free rein and scan new vistas.

Otherwise, work should involve travel, being out and about meeting people, and constantly having to come up with fresh strategies and ideas.

The keys to fulfilment are achievement, challenge and being able to bring about change in the world, or otherwise affect people's lives. Unless the career offers these prospects, there will be a lot of job-hopping through boredom. Self-employment is an excellent idea, because someone with this type of hand might find that corporate structures are too restrictive.

A CREATIVE CAREER

On this hand the inner area is stronger than the outer ❶. The Moon mount is raised and enlarged, the second Mars mount ❷ and the Mercury mount are also significantly strong ❸, and the Sun mount has signs of extra power.

This type of hand signifies a creative and original mind, and one that is open to inspiration and innovation. However, ideas may not be completely thought through and implemented because emotions will run high, and the feelings, including compassion, will be a priority.

Careers and work choices that are linked to creativity and planning are suitable for people with this kind of hand, as is any work that involves problem-solving and developing new visions. Careers in health or in community and conservation fields would also be appropriate.

The owner of this type of hand might find it best to work within a corporate structure rather than launch into self-employment because an element of added discipline is needed to activate practical effort.

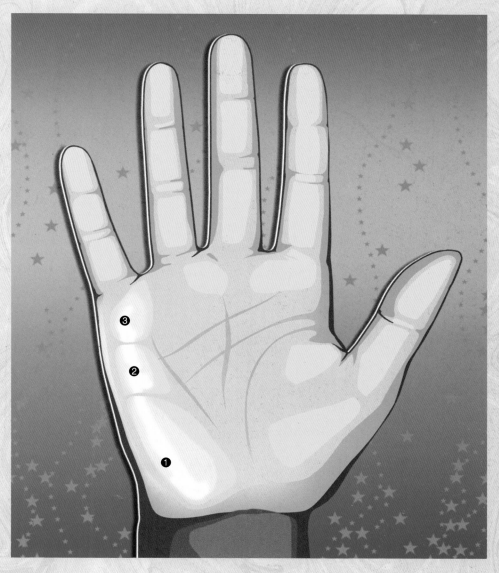

ORIGINAL THINKING ▶

The power and weight of the palm are concentrated in its lower half of this hand. The second and third quarters are dominant, with the weight of the palm in the Venus ❶ and Moon mounts ❷. There is also some development affecting the first and second Mars mounts ❸.

This type of hand reveals a highly creative, innovative and visionary mind. Careers that thrive on innovation, personal energy and a willingness to be original offer the best hopes of achievement and satisfaction to this hand's owner.

The most suitable opportunities would be found within the arts, whether traditional or media-led, and in any industrial or scientific undertaking where new ground needs to be broken and fresh vision brought to bear.

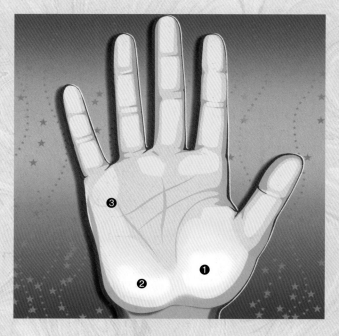

◀ WORKING WITH PEOPLE

The upper half of this palm is well developed, giving the first and third quarters command of the hand. The Jupiter ❶, Saturn ❷, Sun ❸ and Mercury ❹ mounts are all strong and raised.

Someone with a hand like this will have a love of people, new faces and places and also enjoy excellent communications skills. They will have plenty of ambition, but also an easy-going nature, a certain amount of charisma and a character that others find attractive.

The career best suited to people with hands like this must offer high achievement, rapid progress and interaction with other people. Areas of work that revolve around personalities and communication are best and might include any type of sales role, a hairdressing business, education and the media.

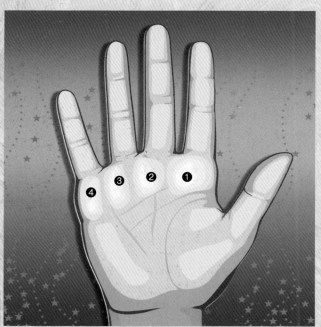

CREATIVE

The first and fourth quarters of this hand are most highly developed. There is a power in the Moon ❶ mount that stretches diagonally across the hand, dipping for the Mars plain but extending into the Jupiter mount ❷ and first Mars mount ❸. The Saturn mount is also affected, albeit to a lesser extent ❹.

This palm will belong to someone who enjoys a busy social life and who loves to be surrounded by beautiful things. Their imagination is important to them, and a career that involves creativity will attract them. Any employment or business that offers contact with the public and uses networking skills would be appropriate, with the media, a career in human resources, the retail sector or the arts all offering excellent chances of success. The energy in the Jupiter mount provides the drive needed to succeed in the competitive worlds of drama or art.

An emotional almost neurotic nature combined with a spark of jealousy will conspire to cause problems with colleagues or employers if these negative tendencies are allowed full rein.

Highly stressed jobs and careers that could bring unpleasant confrontations or difficult situations, such as those involving illness, life-and-death decisions or mundane routine, should be avoided.

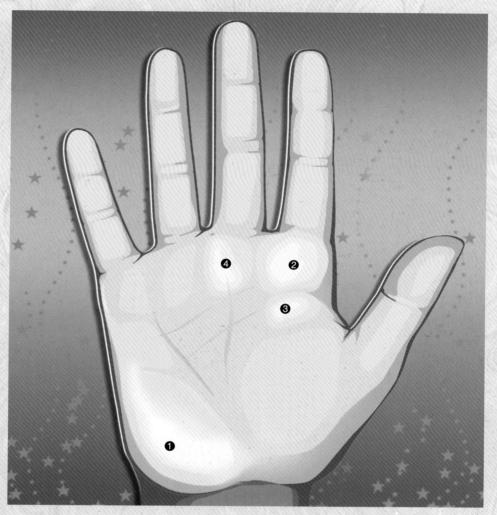

LEADERSHIP QUALITIES

On this palm the second and third quarters are developed. The Venus mount ❶ and first Mars mount are robust ❷, and these are mirrored by strength in the second Mars mount ❸, the Mercury mount ❹ and the Sun mount ❺.

This type of hand indicates energy and would belong to someone who has a career that needs enthusiasm and drive. People-orientated work would be suitable as long as it involved a challenge, such as selling. A person with this type of hand would also find work in medicine, public relations or advertising ideal, and if they wanted a more practical form of employment they should look to construction, transport, gardening or any field that requires passion as well as technique. The characteristics indicated by this type of hand are also ideally suited to work such as childcare or caring or a role that requires

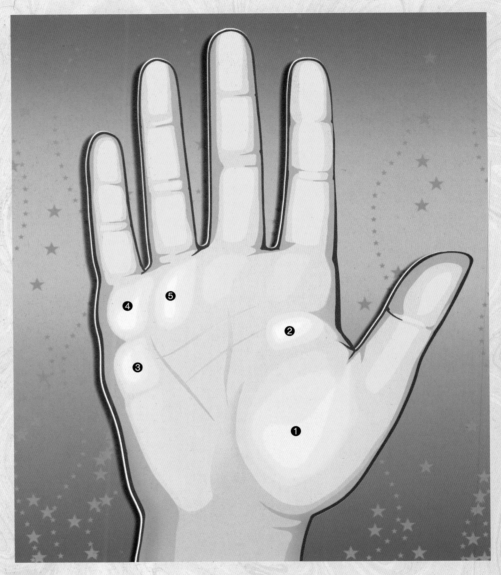

leadership qualities. Self-employment would be a good idea, but it should be in a field that involves contact with the public rather than being tucked away out of sight somewhere.

PUBLIC OPINION COUNTS ▶

The Saturn line begins on the Moon mount ❷ and travels up to end on the Saturn mount.

It is where the line begins that provides a valuable clue to the type of career that will bring success. The Moon mount is the sphere of the Muses and governs imagination, inspiration, creativity and the arts. When the Saturn line begins on the Moon mount it suggests success in a career that depends on public opinion, which could be anything from hairdressing to politics.

When the Saturn line is particularly strong and accompanied by a Sun line, the chosen path will bring fame in music, television, literature or acting, but in these cases there will usually be other signs of creativity and great determination. Look out for a long, sloping head line and a strong-willed thumb.

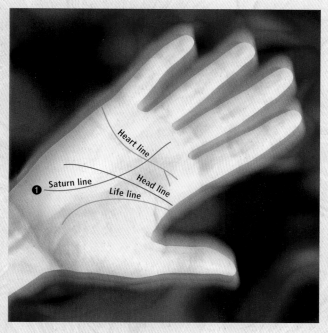

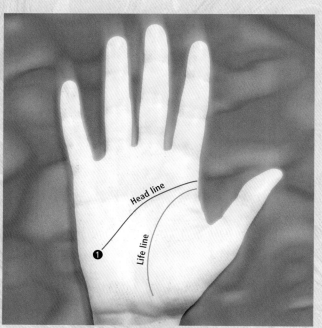

◀ INVENTIVE

A well-formed head line with a slight slope, running down towards the Moon mount ❶, indicates a temperament that is ideal for imaginative work, requiring ideas and innovation. If the hand as a whole is creativity orientated, this could be music, writing or painting. Otherwise, the mind's ability to dream new realities could be turned towards making scientific discoveries, undertaking medical research or designing cars – wherever the passions lie.

To find out which field offers the greatest opportunities, study the mounts and decide which dominates. The careers associated with that mount will need to be assessed to see which excites the imagination. If a career is mentioned that fails to stir your passion, it's definitely the wrong choice.

A WAY WITH WORDS

The head line slopes down the palm towards the Moon mount, suggesting that this person would enjoy careers that involve the use of the imagination or in which the mind can be allowed to create new concepts.

The head line ends in a finely drawn fork on the Moon mount, a configuration that is known as a literary fork and that promises talent in writing imaginative literature. However, it isn't always the mark of a successful novelist. It is commonly found on the hands of all those who make their living by putting pen to paper, ranging from journalists, copywriters and advertising executives to teachers of English. Sometimes the owner of a literary fork uses their word-making ability only briefly; sometimes they do not use it for money but write poetic letters to friends and relatives or make up stories for their children.

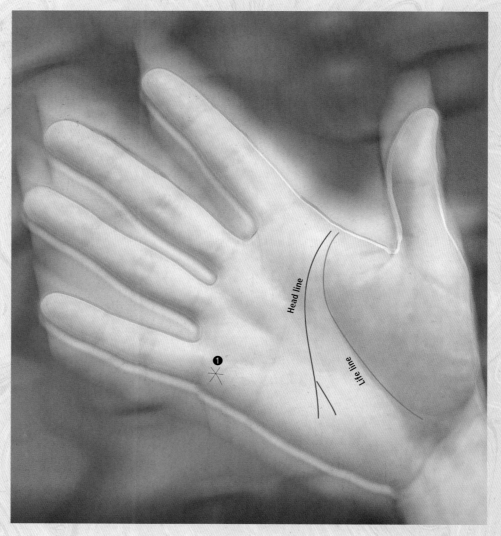

A star at the centre of the Mercury mount ❶ is sometimes found with the literary fork. It's a sign of a brilliant mind and indicates success in science, business or politics or in any capacity that involves making speeches. An off-centre star points to strong links with people who excel in these areas.

A SPIRITUAL PATH

This hand has two fascinating marks. The clear triangle on the Saturn mount is a rare but important sign, indicating a vocational leaning towards mysticism and promising ability in mystical work ❶.

The cross on the Saturn line is called the 'mystical cross' ❷. A cross is a mystical cross only if it appears in what is traditionally known as the quadrangle – that is, the rectangular area between the heart and head lines. A mystical cross that is on the Saturn line or that is actually part of that line suggests that the love of mysticism will influence and help mould the career. The pull towards mysticism could manifest itself as a life devoted to the church, even to the extent of taking holy orders, the study and practice of clairvoyance or hypnotism, or dedication to a healing art with a spiritual base, such as homeopathy, Chinese medicine or even Jungian psychology.

Alternatively, the interest in mysticism could be revealed in a more private way, such as by a lifelong dedication to Buddhism, to Wicca or the practice of the occult. In a creative person this religious, magical sensibility would imbue their art or writing. On the hand of a surgeon or judge it would provide a framework for decision-making and a key to making sense of life's experiences.

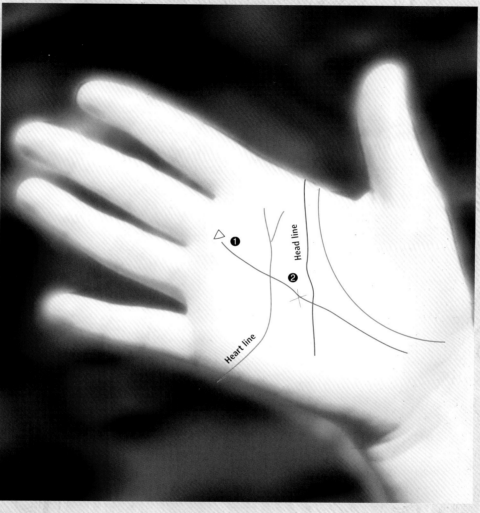

A COMMANDING NATURE

There is a deeply etched triangle on the Jupiter mount of this hand ❶, which indicates a practical and precise ability for organization and planning. This type of triangle is a sign of a natural talent for leadership and the type of charisma that makes commanding others effortless.

Someone with this triangle would find success in careers that include management, business, the civil service, sometimes the church and at officer rank in the military or other services. If the hand has signs of literary talents, the person could also be the editor of a newspaper or magazine.

The spearhead ❷ promises exceptional success in whatever fields are symbolized by the mount on which it appears. Here, on the first Mars mount, it suggests that there would be distinction in military service, the police and emergency services, sport or handling dangerous materials (such as nuclear fuel) – anything, in fact, that calls for strategy, courage and a cool mind in a crisis.

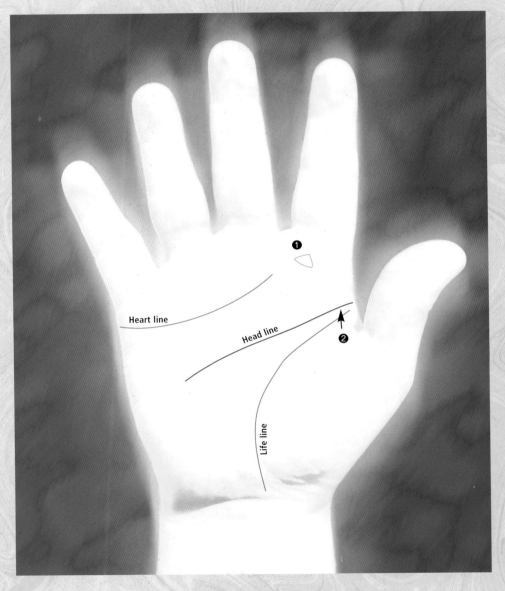

Heart line

Head line

Life line

TALENT WINS ▶

There are two triangles on this hand, and although they complement each other, they are not always found together on the same palm.

The triangle on the Sun mount is a promising omen ❶, signifying talent and success in an artistic field and a non-egotistical attitude towards recognition and fame. Money, attention and respect will be won, but they will not spoil or damage the personality. Someone with this triangle is able to remain balanced under pressure.

A triangle on the Moon mount ❷ gives a highly creative imagination. Inspiration will not be wasted but will be transformed into reality, being used to produce art, music, literature or poetry or new inventions. Such a triangle will not always mean that a career requiring creativity will be chosen, but it may do so.

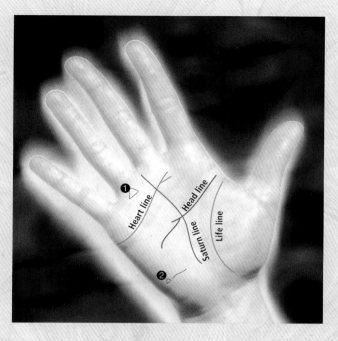

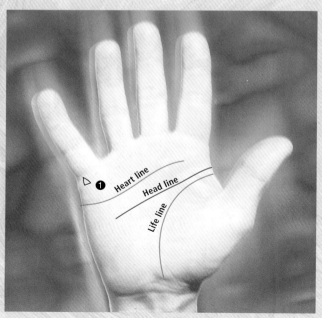

◀ A WINNING TRADER

A triangle is always a mark of aptitude and success. On this hand it is displayed on the Mercury mount ❶, where it is an emblem of an excellent mind for business, whether in the world of high finance or buying and selling motor vehicles. There will be a natural inclination towards doing deals, and someone with this mark on their hand will get a real buzz when a bargain or sale is tied up.

As long as the rest of the palm is balanced, the triangle suggests that money will be made. The actual field of success may be financial, such as the stock market, pawn-broking, banking or speculating in gold, diamonds or currency. It also speaks of a head for figures, and a person with this sign will understand money and know how to manipulate it to create wealth.

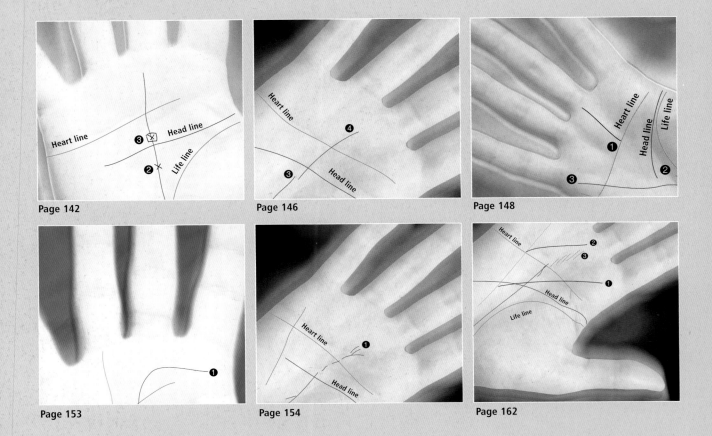

Page 142

Heart line   **❸** ⊠   Head line

❷ ✕   Life line

Page 146

Heart line

❹

❸   Head line

Page 148

Heart line

Head line

Life line

❶

❷

❸

Page 153

❶

Page 154

Heart line

❶

Head line

Page 162

Heart line

❷

❸

❶

Head line

Life line

IIn these pagés you'll be able to trace the progress of your career, gain a clue as to the status you'll achieve, and get a glimpse at your future financial security. Your story could be simple or complicated, successful or challenging.

How Will My Career Develop?

9

How Will My Career Develop?

Everyone desires to discover how well they are going to do in life, the status they will achieve, the money they will make and when breakthroughs are going to come.

No matter how we define and measure success – by reaching an artistic peak, attaining celebrity, healing others, making a difference in the community, safeguarding the natural world or just providing a good home and safe family environment – everything is on the palm.

The way a career develops through the years is mapped out on the palm, and here the Saturn line is the most important guide. Usually beginning near the wrist, the line flows up the hand, telling the story of gains and losses, successes and defeats. The Sun line reveals extra information, and the life line holds secrets, too.

All the events in your working, business or creative life can be pinpointed by checking with the palm's built-in dating system (see page 89). For happenings on the life line, read the date from the life line. The same holds true for the Saturn line.

The better drawn the Saturn line is, the more success it promises. To judge its strength correctly, first examine the depth of the head line, heart line, Mercury line and life line. If the Saturn line is stronger than these, the level of your wealth and status will be high. When these lines are of the same strength, your material lifestyle will be comfortable. When the Saturn line is weaker than the other lines, determined action will be needed to make sure that money and resources are adequate.

Does my hand shape affect my career?

- As we have already seen, hand shape does affect a person's career. It also determines character and therefore pinpoints areas for a successful career. In addition, Saturn, Mars and Sun hands can be more determined and, therefore, more likely to succeed, while Mercury, Moon and Venus hands often find it more of a challenge to get to the top.
- The stronger, straighter and longer your Saturn line is, the better your prospects are.
- However, to ensure success, a Saturn line on a Mercury, Moon or Venus hand has to be more powerful than on a Saturn, Mars or Sun hand.

THE SUN LINE

The Sun line is also known as the Apollo line, fortune line or success line. It is one of the most mysterious paths on the palm, relating not only to worldly fortune and the acquisition of money, power, celebrity and respect from others but also to artistic gifts and the ability to appreciate beauty in all its forms.

The Sun line works in combination with the Saturn line, and a strong Sun line will help compensate for a weaker Saturn line. The Sun line is like the cream on the cake. The Saturn line symbolizes all the hard work that is put into a career, while the Sun line gives the rewards and recognition and, strangely, the knack of enjoying money and its benefits. Financial security, of course, provides the leisure time necessary to enjoy the arts or even to take part in them.

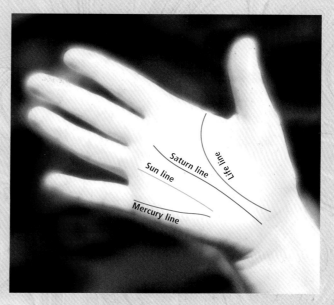

Not all Sun lines are deep and long, but most people have a trace of one. The better marked it is and the fewer breaks, islands and other interruptions there are, the more powerful it is. When you gauge the line's strength the hand shape must also be taken into account. Hand shapes that are more receptive to beauty – Venus, Mercury and Moon hands – always have Sun lines that are more strongly shown than on the less imaginative and more pragmatic hand shapes – that is, those of Sun, Saturn and Mars. While a solid Sun line on a Venus hand will bring success, therefore, much of its power will enhance aesthetic values and good taste. However, a weaker Sun line on a Saturn hand will bring just as much achievement and renown.

In practical terms, the Sun line works in much the same way as the Saturn line. The key difference is that the Saturn line represents material fortune, while the Sun line symbolizes the reputation and celebrity that material prosperity brings. Not everyone will become famous – nor, indeed, will they seek to be famous – but we all like to be respected and known for what we do. After all, a greengrocer can be famous locally for the size and freshness of his cabbages.

When you are dating events on the Sun line, base the calculations on the Saturn line. Look across from the branch, break or other marking on the Sun line and judge what age the Saturn line shows at a point exactly parallel to this. This will also be the age at which the event takes place on the Sun line.

Not everyone has a Sun line. If it is missing it is a warning that no matter how talented you are, unless you alter your life strategy and ways of thinking, you will not achieve too much and your abilities will never be recognized. You may, of course, be happy with this – who knows?

SUCCESS

This hand boasts the perfect Saturn line. It begins just above the centre of the wrist, a sign of good fortune, and runs straight up the hand to the Saturn mount. It is deep and strong, never deviating from its path. This signifies great success. When the Saturn line ends on the Saturn mount it is a sign that, ultimately, the person's destiny will be fulfilled and they will succeed in their career and achieve financial stability.

It is said that if the Saturn line begins from below the first bracelet, talents, traits and attitudes formed in a past life will be brought into play and used during the current incarnation.

This hand shows a single influence line running from the Moon mount and joining the Saturn line ❶. This reveals that strong influence from another person – a friend, employer, patron, lover or family member – will provide an opportunity for career advancement or give encouragement and inspiration. This effect begins at the point the influence line meets the Saturn line. In the hand illustrated this would be at the age of 30.

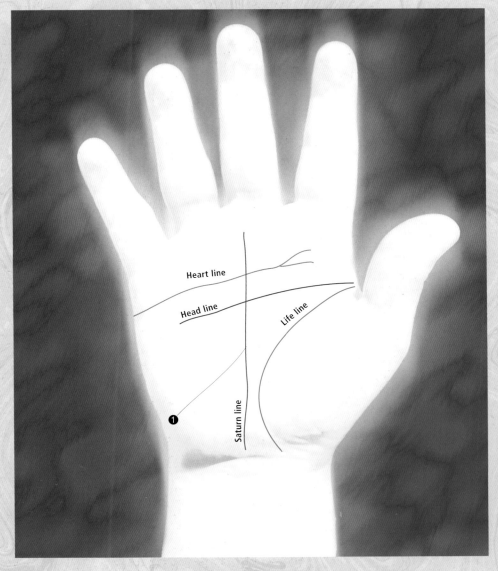

Heart line

Head line

Life line

Saturn line

❶

TRIUMPH OVER STRUGGLES

The Saturn line on this hand begins within the life line on the Venus mount, from where it runs up the hand to the Saturn mount, promising a good career and achievement. On its journey, however, the line becomes chained in two places.

The thumb side of the hand is known as the family side; the Mercury finger's side is the friends' side. A Saturn line emerging from within the life line ❶ symbolizes that the person's early life was dominated and influenced by the wishes of their parents or guardians. This isn't necessarily a bad thing, and unless the beginning of the Saturn line is marred by islands, chains, severe weakness or breaks, it speaks of a sheltered but loving family during childhood.

This changes when the Saturn line emerges from the life line on to the palm. At this point, which can be dated from Saturn line, a new, individual path is taken, which, on the hand illustrated, occurs at the age of 21. The new path does not necessarily mean that there was a rift

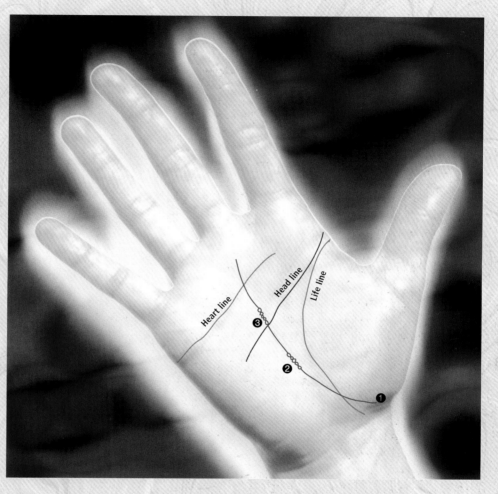

with the family; it is just that the career chosen was not a family occupation and was not selected by the family.

The chains on the Saturn line are signs of struggles, difficult work conditions and periods when it was necessary to fight for recognition and reward. These phases can be dated from the Saturn line as lasting from age 28 to 35 ❷ and 41 to 42 ❸.

CONQUERING A BAD START

On this hand the Saturn line begins within the life line on the Venus mount, showing that this person was dominated by their parents or guardians until they were 22 years old. Unfortunately, while it remains on the Venus mount, the Saturn line is broken in several places and is marked with two islands ❶.

Breaks in the Saturn line relate to setbacks in a person's career. When they are seen early in life they reveal difficulties in someone's emotional development or education. All islands signify phases of loss through adversity and conflict. Luckily, once the Saturn line leaves the life line and becomes free of this bad start, the fortune improves.

The cross, pinpointed on the Saturn line at about the age of 35 ❷, indicates a further period of trouble, leading to a downturn in progress and a loss of financial status. The Saturn line continues just as strongly after the cross, however, and this shows that there was a complete recovery from these setbacks.

The second cross, which is imprisoned within a square ❸, indicates a challenge or problem at the age of 48 that could have led to loss of money and status. Fortunately, squares are signs of preservation, and in this case, the square protects the person from any setbacks and losses the cross may have represented. It is possible that valuable lessons were learned at the time the first cross had its effect.

Overall, this hand is an example of the triumph of the human spirit. No matter how bad someone's start in life may be, they can overcome its effects and fulfil their destiny.

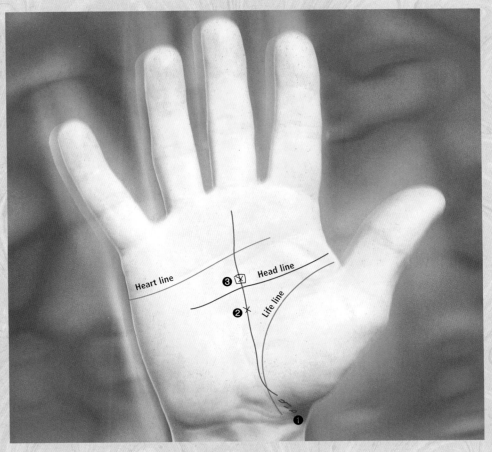

Heart line
Head line
Life line
❸ ❷ ❶

LOVE EMPOWERS

The Saturn line here does not begin within the life line on the Venus mount. Instead, it starts below the life line and hugs it closely for part of its journey up the palm ❶, before veering away and eventually reaching the Saturn mount.

An influence line crosses from the Moon mount and reaches the Saturn line but ends in an island ❷. A second influence line travels from the Moon mount, turns upwards and ascends alongside the Saturn line ❸.

A Saturn line that begins below the life line and follows it for a distance shows that the person's career and life are moulded by the influence and wishes of parents and relatives. When the line begins to veer away it shows that independence is asserted and that an individual life path has begun. Even when the Saturn line shadows the life line, the family may not be forcefully oppressive but merely express narrow views or be overprotective.

The first influence line ends in an island, which tells of a relationship that causes a fall in status and wealth.

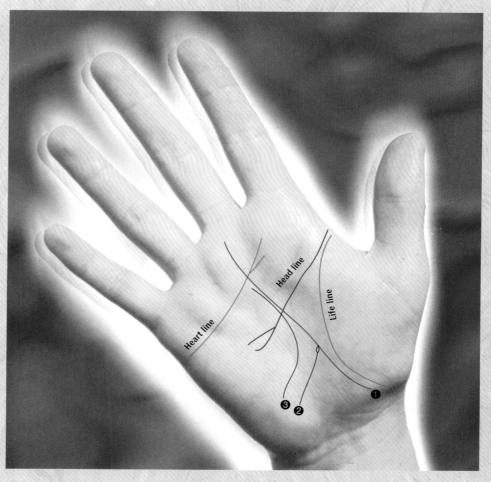

The second influence line is more positive. Running close to the Saturn line, it indicates that this person will meet a partner, husband or wife, whose support, influence, wealth or social position helps their career to flourish. The relationship begins when the influence line turns upwards at the side of the Saturn line. On the hand illustrated this was around the age of 33.

AN UNFORTUNATE UNION

Every hand tells a story. The tale revealed in this hand revolves around an otherwise excellent Saturn line, which begins on the thumb's side of the hand and then straightens up, before stopping short at the heart line as if the upper portion had been removed ❶. There is also a break in the Saturn line further down.

When the Saturn line is born on the thumb or family side of the hand, the influence of family and society as a whole will play a significant role in a person's fate.

If the Saturn line is cut short by the heart line, it is always because the emotions or a particular relationship ruin the career and any chances of success. This can be the result of the sacrifices made for love, a scandal caused by an affair, the influence of a dissolute lover or a mental illness provoked by an unhappy affair. It can also be caused by someone adopting a non-evolutionary lifestyle to suit a partner.

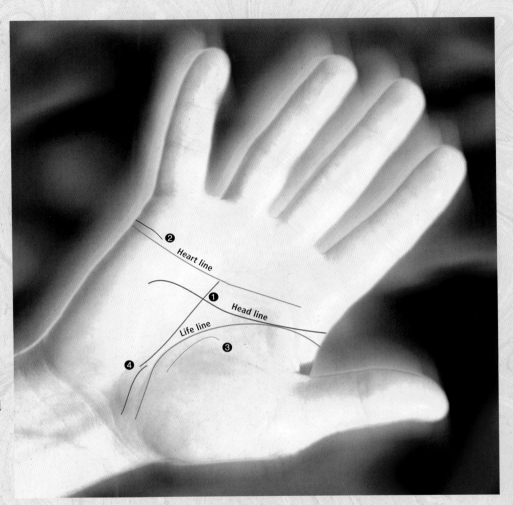

The unfortunate relationship can be found on the Mercury mount ❷, and it is also represented by an influence line on the Venus mount ❸. In addition, the break in the Saturn line, a sign of money loss and demotion, occurs at around 26 ❹, the same age as the relationship line on the Mercury mount begins . This can also be dated from the influence line's position on the life line.

A TROUBLED PATH

This Saturn line begins on the Mercury finger's or friends' side of the hand ❶, indicating that friends and other outside influences hold much more sway over the person's imagination and career choices than any family member. The Saturn line does straighten up, hinting that some of these influences fall away as individuality and original thinking begin to assert themselves.

When the Saturn line veers completely across the hand towards the thumb side, it would mean that family influences have overtaken outside ones. This can also work the other way round.

The Saturn line illustrated becomes chained as it progresses ❷, a mark of challenges to the person's position in life, power struggles at work and a lack of appreciation from colleagues, employers or clients.

It is unfortunate when a Saturn line is stopped by the head line: this is an indication of a career halted by a rash, stupid, or badly thought-out action or project. This could arise through grave financial miscalculation or by being cheated by fraudsters. In some cases, where there are clear

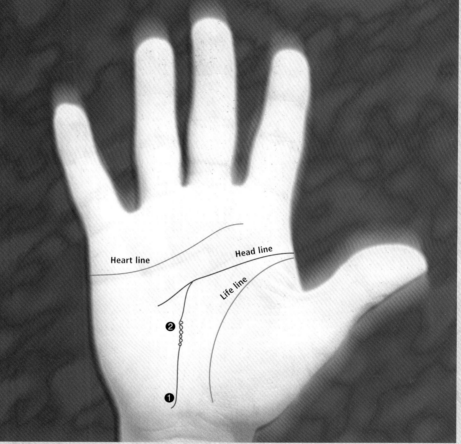

signs of mental imbalance on the hand, a breakdown or period of mental illness could be the cause (see Chapter 10 and also check the head line).

The story of the hand illustrated can be easily read. The struggles revealed by the extended chain lead to one final desperate business or job-hopping gamble, which goes wrong and causes ruin. Bankruptcy normally accompanies a Saturn line that is stemmed by the head line.

A CHANGE OF CAREER

The Saturn line illustrated here begins with a fork ❶, one branch of which is on the Moon mount, the other being near the Venus mount. This arrangement indicates a passionate nature and wild imagination, with love switching from family and friends to the arts. The fortunes will be founded on, or destroyed by, the effects of both, but here there will be success because the Saturn line has depth and reaches the Saturn mount.

The first break, which occurs at the age of 30, displays a career setback ❷. In practice this can mean the termination of someone's employment or a period of rest period, which will last as long as the break lasts. Once the Saturn line begins again, new work is started.

The second break takes place at the age of 33 or 34 ❸. A new Saturn line actually begins just before the break and continues up the palm, where it is even stronger than the first line ❹. This is a symbol of a complete and radical career transformation. It also rules out the previous break having been a period of rest.

That the new career is more successful than the first is shown by the fact that the second Saturn line grows in power as it progresses. If the second Saturn line was weaker than the first, the new work path would be less in harmony with the self and provide fewer rewards.

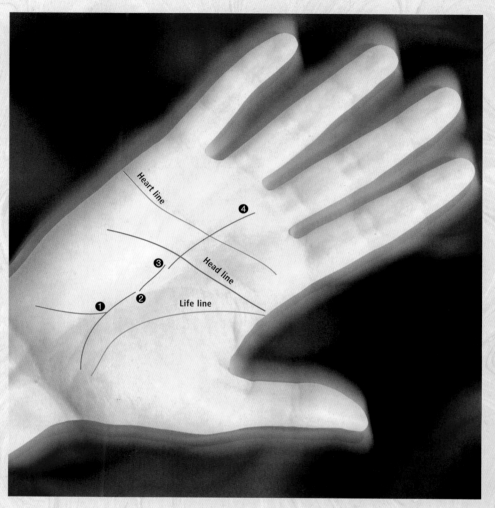

Heart line
Head line
Life line
❶ ❷ ❸ ❹

STABILITY AFTER STRUGGLE

Fascinatingly, the Saturn line on this palm emerges from the head line ❶, promising achievement after a fierce and long struggle. A person showing this configuration will have succeeded entirely through their own hard, dedicated work and by strongly relying on their natural talents. They will have achieved financial security and a reasonable status only after the age of 35. There are usually other indications on the palm to pinpoint how and when this progress was made.

A branch leaving the Saturn line and ascending the palm to join the Mercury line ❷ points to business success or promotion in a career that is linked to Mercury, such as import and export, travel, education, media or science. Work out the timing from the point the branch leaves the Saturn line. In this instance it is the age of 41.

There is also a second, weaker Saturn line shadowing the first above the head line ❸. This second line has breaks in it. A second Saturn line represents a second business or job, conducted at the same time as the first. When the second line is much weaker, as it is here, it shows an employment or business venture that is less important. The breaks shown may

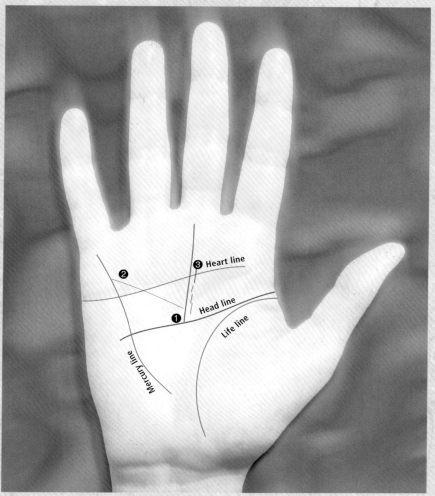

indicate that this second business was meant to replace the main career but that it failed to take off as planned, because of difficulties and periods of inactivity.

On some hands the second, weaker Saturn line is a 'hobby' job or business, such as pottery or growing dahlias, which is done just for fun.

ACHIEVEMENT LATER IN LIFE ▶

This Saturn line rises from the heart line ❶, pointing to a long and difficult struggle to achieve the ambitions. This person attained their desires around the age of 56. This later success will be more in harmony with the inner nature than if victory had been gained earlier in life.

Lines ascending from the life line are marks of increase in power, rank or success. Here the position of the little rising lines ❷ add support to the Saturn line's prediction of attainment in later life.

The longer branch from the life line to the Mercury mount ❸ suggests that this late triumph will be in a career linked to Mercury, such as the media, science, education, politics or technology or anything that involves communication. A branch like this is always weaker than the Mercury line.

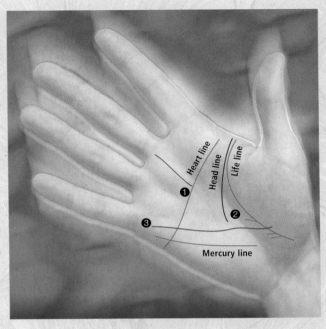

◀ TWO CAREERS

This unusual hand has a Saturn line beginning quite high up the palm ❶. The line can begin at any point and its appearance marks the time when career success begins and the rewards of effort are realized.

Here the Saturn line appears at around the age of 31, when the career really takes off. The fine ascending lines rising from the life line ❷, also show promotions, extra income and recognition.

The second Saturn line is as strong as the first ❸. This suggests a second career as successful as the first, except for a 'rest', indicated by the tiny break ❹. This second business or profession would be different from the first, although it could be linked to it – for example, an English teacher might also be a successful novelist or an engineer might race cars and win.

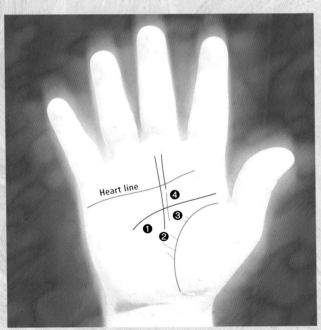

THE PATH TO FORTUNE

This hand looks complicated, but it is simpler than it seems. The Saturn line is wavy, undulating its way up towards the Saturn mount 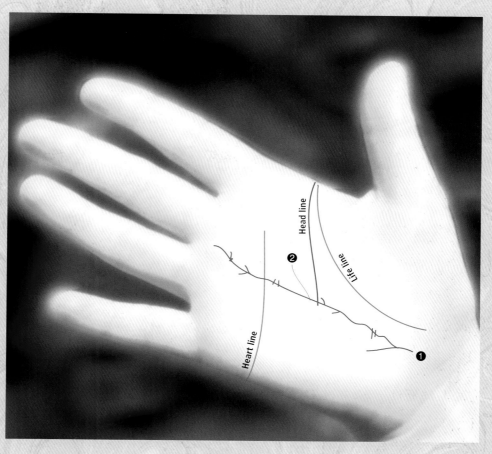. Here and there short bars cross the line. In other places fine lines leave the Saturn line and begin to ascend the palm. One line, which is longer than the others, leaves the Saturn line and runs part of the way towards the Jupiter mount ❷.

The short bars are obstacles, sometimes the influence or activities of other people. They hinder and make progress difficult. Nevertheless, the Saturn line continues on its way, showing that these barriers have been overcome. If ever a bar stops a Saturn line in its progress, that obstacle has successfully ended the person's career.

The wavy parts of this Saturn line symbolize ups and downs in the person's fortune – in other words, they indicate that there have been struggles before success.

The fine lines that periodically rise from the Saturn line are marks of good fortune. Each describes a promotion, a step forwards or a little extra income. The stronger these lines are, the greater the advance or increase in recognition or revenue.

The longer and stronger line that runs part way to the Jupiter mount of this hand, represents a significant success in a career that is associated with Jupiter. This could be in the leisure industry, the money markets, big business, entertainment or politics, including local government.

Both blocks and rising lines can be dated from the Saturn line.

CHARISMA EASES THE WAY

There's a lot going on this hand. The way to approach reading a palm is to analyse each little line individually and to weigh them up as a whole before drawing any conclusions.

The Saturn line illustrated here is fairly good ❶. However, it is complicated here and there by tiny lines leaving it and running down the palm ❷. Each of these represents a fall in rank, a cut in salary or actual loss of money.

The influence lines that arise on the Venus mount within the life line and run out across the palm to cut the Saturn line reveal people who oppose progress in career or business ❸. They can be malicious relatives, business competitors, jealous colleagues, selfish lovers or overprotective parents. The date at which they negatively affect the person's work can be judged from the point at which they cross the Saturn line.

It is one of the rules of palmistry that any line that crosses another, weakens it, while any line that merges with another strengthens it.

A firm branch leaves the Saturn line at around the age of 34 and runs towards the Sun mount ❹. This is a mark of a step forwards in a field linked to the Sun, and it could involve a move into the limelight or an achievement revolving around the

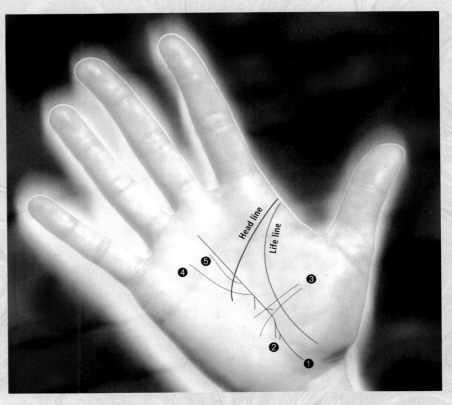

arts, crafts, construction, the retail sector, advertising or events organization – anything, in fact, that relies on personal charisma to make it work.

Just beyond this branch a second Saturn line emerges from the first and travels upwards alongside it ❺. This is a second career or business that has developed organically from the first. It continues in harmony with the first occupation, and together they create better fortune. When the line stops, the second venture ceases. An example would be a florist who decides to branch out into growing flowers or an estate agent who tackles some property development.

A SECURE RETIREMENT ▶

A branch leaves the Saturn line and travels part of the way towards the Mercury mount ❶. This indicates advancement in a Mercury-related field, such as communications, travel, sales or education. To judge when this happens, study the Saturn line.

A long branch rises from the life line and flows to the Jupiter mount ❷. Its position on the life line indicates an ambition fulfilled and achievement of a position of power at around the age of 56.

Little lines rising and falling from the Saturn line represent the usual ups and downs of a working life. A large island mars the Saturn line between the ages of 30 and 33 ❸, suggesting a period of adversity and financial hardship. However, a short Sun line on the Sun mount ❹ promises that there will be wealth and security in old age.

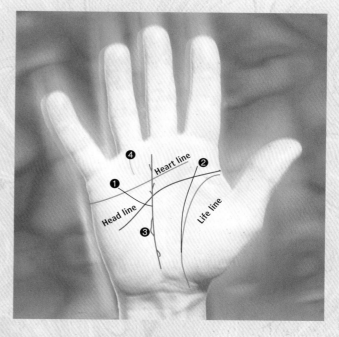

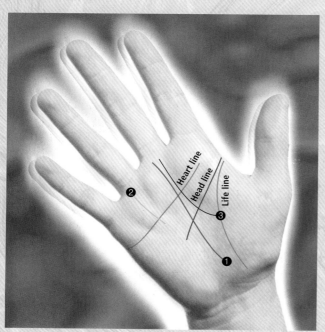

◀ GAINS MADE EARLY

The Saturn line here shows success ❶. A healthy Sun line appears between the head and the heart line ❷, indicating that after the age of 40, through their intelligence and effort, the person will enjoy achievement and win respect from others.

This attainment has its roots earlier on. A strong line leaves the life line and flows onto the Saturn mount ❸, promising a significant increase of wealth, achieved through the acquisition of property, land or companies. The time of this good fortune has to be divined from the life line, and on the hand illustrated it is at the age of 26.

Although money comes relatively early, the later appearance of the Sun line suggests that respect and recognition are not the result of the gains made when the person was in their 20s but were won by further hard work later in life.

A POSITION OF RESPECT

There is power in this palm. A deep Saturn line sweeps across the palm, ending on the Jupiter mount rather than on the Saturn mount ❶. This reveals immense inner drive, ambition and determination, and indicates that there will be success, recognition in the public eye and power over other people's lives. This is the mark of a highly placed politician, a media mogul, a captain of industry, a general or an entrepreneur. Tellingly, this pinnacle is reached through individual effort and vision, whether the life began in poverty or in riches.

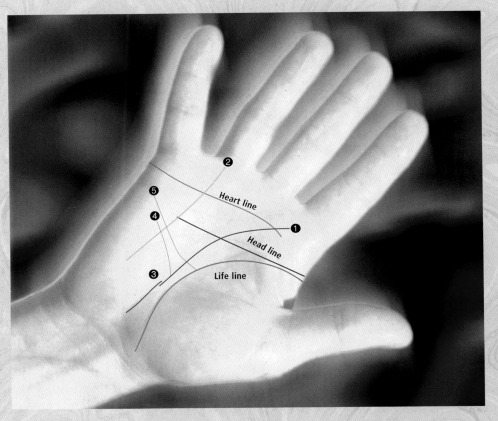

A long, strong Sun line adds to this picture ❷, showing that success and the fruits of success will be enjoyed. The line begins on the Moon mount, which is a mark of someone whose fortune depends on public support. On a creative hand this would point to an actor or musician. Here, it is more likely to be the badge of a politician.

A break in the Saturn line earlier in life tells of a change of career and tactics on this road to power ❸.

Clues to the field of achievement are given by a branch line that leaves the Saturn line and runs towards the second Mars mount. This represents promotion in a role associated with the second Mars mount ❹ at around the age of 30.

Similarly, a firm branch leaves the life line and crosses to the second Mars mount ❺, revealing that when they were 28 years old the person made a leap forward on a career path associated with the second Mars mount. This could be in law, politics, the civil service, health or anything that benefits the community and makes a difference to society.

Date these branches from when they leave either the Saturn line or the life line.

A CHANGE IN DESTINY

This is a remarkable hand. A good, productive Saturn line travels up the hand to the Saturn mount, where it turns and crosses to the Jupiter mount before ending. This is the mark of an individual who, through a supreme effort, has literally changed their destiny and reached the highest peak their career can offer 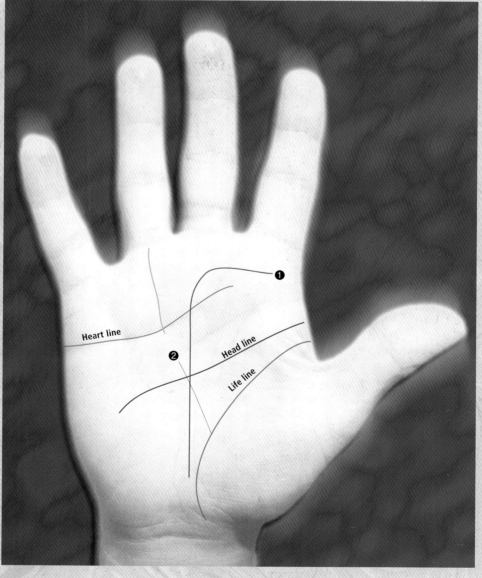.

A branch runs from the life line and heads towards the Sun mount ❷, representing a time when recognition or an award is given for achievement, either academically or in a work-related sphere. This happens when the person was 45 years old. This could have been the breakthrough and inspiration for the immense effort that eventually changed the path of the Saturn line.

The Sun line begins below the heart line, signifying that success will arrive and be enjoyed, but only after struggles and sadness.

Heart line

Head line

Life line

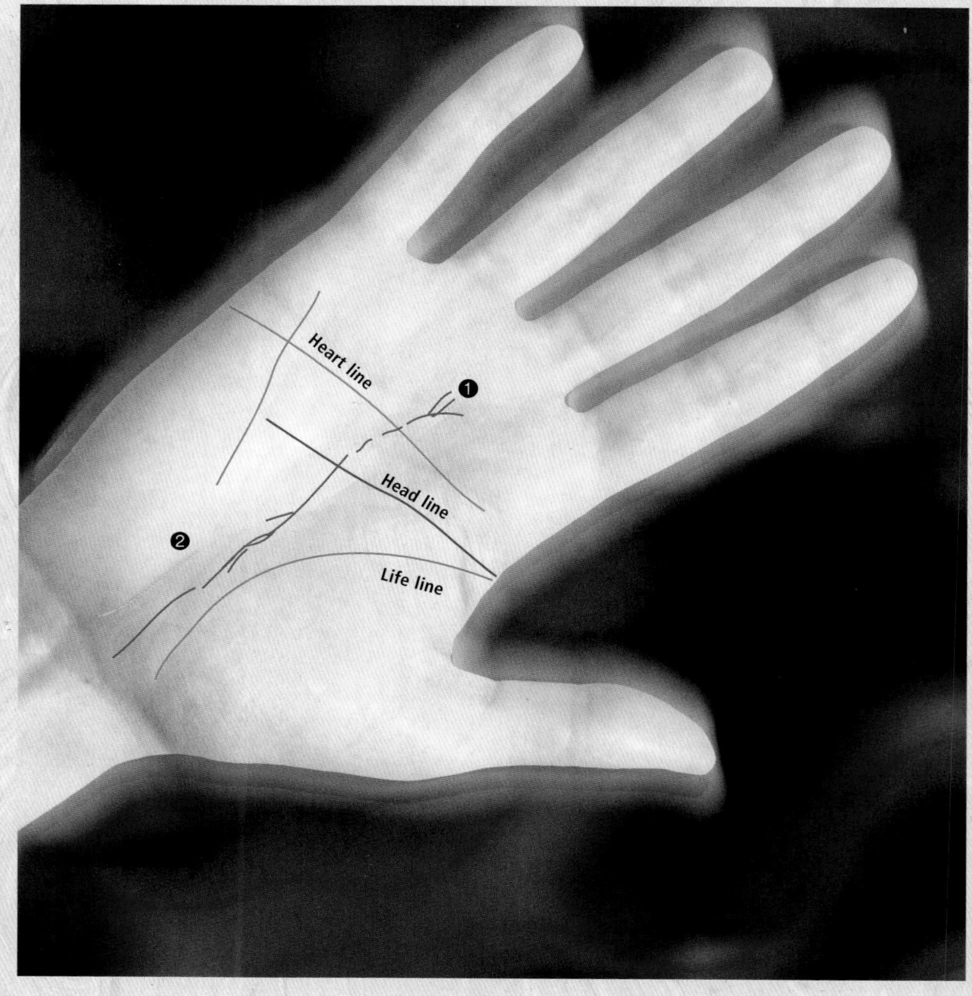

WASTED TALENT

This hand is less promising. The Saturn line is interrupted by periods of misfortune, which are represented by islands and fine descending lines, and there are also plenty of breaks in it ❶. These signify changes in employment, but none of these new opportunities improves the line by making it stronger, so none of them brings success. The Saturn line ends in several weak little lines, indicating that the energies are wasted in a number of fruitless projects.

The Sun line is also far from ideal ❷. Beginning strongly at the wrist, it displays talent but soon runs out of steam, indicating that early promise is unfulfilled and that the career comes to nothing. This is because of a lack of perseverance. This person's natural abilities are not promoted or practised enough to bring recognition. If you have this mark on your hand, stick with your chosen career path and use your natural abilities. You can change your lines if you put effort into your life.

Heart line

Head line

Life line

HEALTH TROUBLES

The wavy Saturn line on this hand reveals times of variable success, sometimes up, sometimes down. The line also stops short of the Saturn mount ❶, suggesting that the person will never achieve their full career potential. The reason for these troubles can be seen in the lines falling from the Saturn line and running to the Mercury line ❷. These indicate demotion, a decline in respect from others and losses of money or periods when earning an income was not possible. These adverse conditions are caused by ill-health, which may be a physical or mental illness, such as a nervous breakdown. It should be possible to diagnose the person's health problems by studying other features on the hand (see Chapter 10).

The Sun line generally supports this tale of misfortune. It appears later on, above the head line ❸, suggesting that any advances that are made take place after the age of 40. However, the line is broken in several places, and most of the breaks are gaps showing periods when the person was out of work or unable to

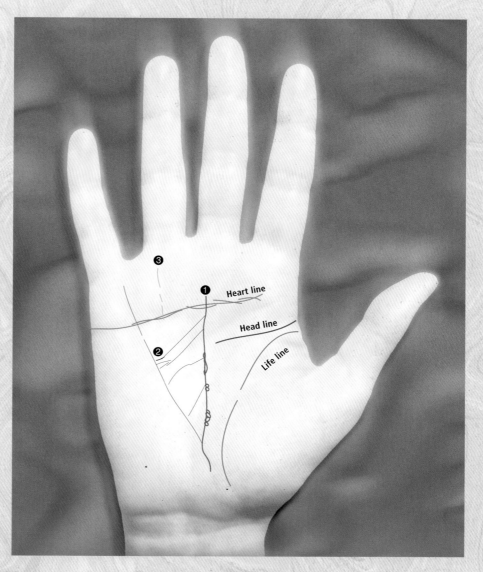

work. When there is a break in a Sun line, and a new Sun line begins before the break, a fresh career path is found but there is no rest period between the two.

HIGH OFFICE ▶

A powerful branch leaves the Saturn line and travels up to the Jupiter mount ❶. This indicates an award, promotion or ascension to a position of power, taking place at the time indicated by the point the branch leaves the Saturn line. This mark occurs on the palms of determined people, who seek high status and public office. In this case, the leap to power happens at the age of 42.

The Sun line begins from the heart line ❷, so the pinnacle of wealth and social standing takes place between the ages of 49 and 56. The line is deep and straight, so finances will be secure.

The head line is straight and strong, indicating a good intellect, and, given the Sun line's blessings, it is likely to be focused on position in society and the trappings of wealth than on creativity and the arts.

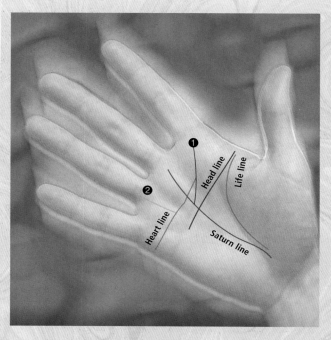

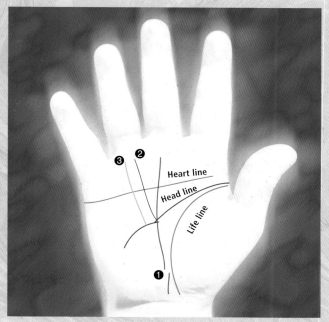

◀ IN THE PUBLIC GAZE

A break early on the Saturn line tells of a career switch ❶. A branch from the Saturn line ascends the palm and reaches the Sun mount ❷. Estimated from the Saturn line's built-in dating system, this can be dated to the age of 35 and it indicates a step into the public eye. This could be a career advancement that attracts attention or the beginning of acclaim within the arts. As the Saturn line stays steady, the ambitions will stay focused on this area.

The Sun line rises from the head line and runs to the Sun mount ❸, showing that renown and satisfaction will come after 35 and will be achieved solely through the person's own natural gifts, effort and intelligence.

The head line is long and curving. This and the Sun line will mean that the arts will be appreciated and patronized.

EXCELLENT FORTUNE

A Sun line ending in a trident on the Sun mount promises great wealth, success and the fulfilment of ambitions ❶. It is even more significant when it is on such a long, deep Sun line. This excellent fortune will be made possible by individual effort and through the thoughtful channelling of mental powers.

Always look elsewhere on the hand for clues about the type of career that would provide the setting for triumph. On this hand a firm branch line leaves the Saturn line and terminates at the centre of the Mercury mount ❷. It speaks of an advantageous step into a career that is linked to Mercury, which could be in business, science, computers, communications, lecturing, journalism or even weather forecasting.

The branch that runs to the Mercury mount cannot be confused with the Mercury line, which can be seen crossing the Saturn line on its journey down the hand ❸.

The Saturn line also displays a break at around the same period ❹. This supports the view that this new path into a Mercury-related sphere is a complete change from a previous type of employment.

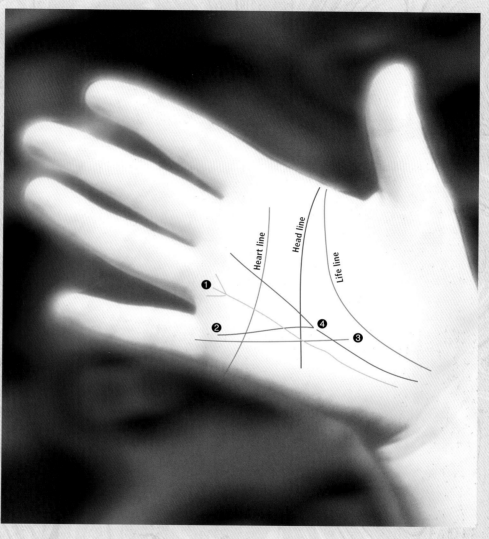

Heart line
Head line
Life line

PUBLIC SERVICE

This hand has some interesting marks. The Saturn line begins from the Moon mount ❶, hinting that the career will be in a public field or, at least, in a profession that depends on public support. Just above the head line a firm branch veers away and terminates in the middle of the second Mars mount ❷. This is an indication of a move into a career that is associated with the second Mars mount, which could be in the civil service, the legal profession, a human rights organization, nursing or the fire brigade – anything, in short, where the focus is on providing a service and improving the quality of life for other people.

The new career flourishes. This is shown by the clearly marked star on the Sun line ❸.

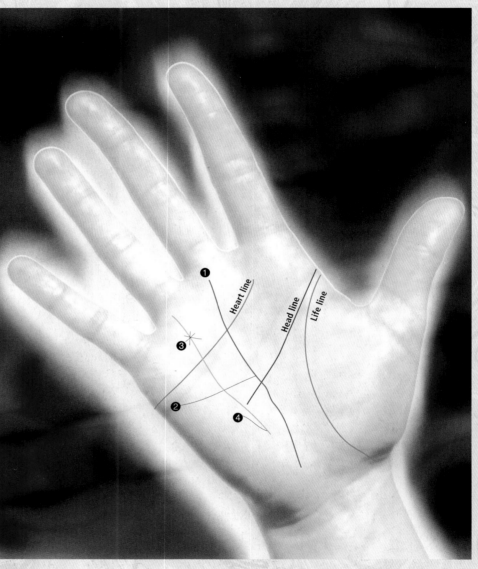

Wherever a star appears on a Sun line it indicates a spell of brilliance and lasting success.

There is also a secondary Sun line, which emerges from the original Sun line ❹and follows it up the hand for a little while. This represents a new venture or creative enterprise, which will be successful and give satisfaction but will never rival the main career.

A MILITARY LIFE

The Saturn line on this hand is long and well developed, suggesting that the person's career will be successful ❶. Towards its end it veers over to the Jupiter mount but terminates just short of it, between the Jupiter finger and the Saturn finger. This is an indication that the person expended immense personal willpower to achieve their goals. Their effort was rewarded.

A strong branch leaves the Saturn line at the age of 32 and travels to the first Mars mount ❷. This points to advancement in a profession that is associated with that mount, such as sport, the police, exploration, foundry work or the military. This hand bears further clues to the precise career that was chosen. There is a square sitting on the life line under the Jupiter mount, a sign of active service before the age of 20 ❸. Squares are symbols of preservation; in this case, from death in battle. In addition, there is a distinct star on the second Mars mount ❹. This is a sign of promotion to high military rank or of decoration for bravery; it also shows that the person saw service in one or more significant battles during a major war or conflict.

The owner of this hand definitely chose a military career. Active service after the age of 20 is shown in other ways, usually by a square on the Venus mount, with a cross at it centre and a line

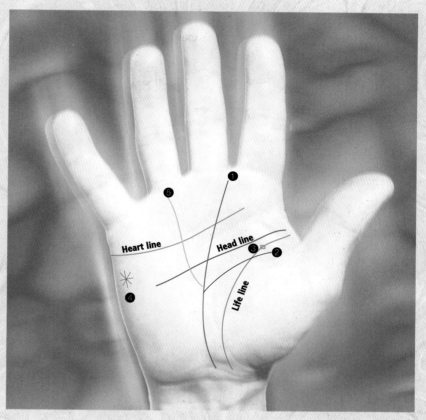

running from the square to the second Mars mount.

The Sun line actually emerges from the Saturn line ❺. It can be easily distinguished from a branch running to the Sun mount by its strength. The Sun line will usually be almost as deeply marked as the Saturn line or any of the other major palm lines. The point at which the Sun line leaves the Saturn mount is the time from which life vastly improves, with funds accumulating and respect being gained. On this military hand this would suggest another rise in rank, which takes place shortly after the first promotion at the age of 34.

A LUCKY CAREER CHANGE

The Sun line on this hand is born from the life line ❶. It is easy to tell the difference between a true Sun line and a branch thrown from the life line to the Sun mount. The Sun line will be better marked than any branch line.

A Sun line that begins from the life line on a Venus, Mercury, Moon or refined Sun hand reveals a life devoted to art and the fine things of life. Success in an artistic field is likely if the Saturn line is also good, the Moon mount is pronounced and other signs of creativity are present. A Sun line that rises from the life line on a coarser Sun, Saturn or Mars hand shows a life dedicated to forging ahead in a career, carving a reputation and making money. In both cases, the point at which the Sun line leaves the life line gives the date when the life's work began in earnest. On this hand it is fairly late in life, at the age of 52.

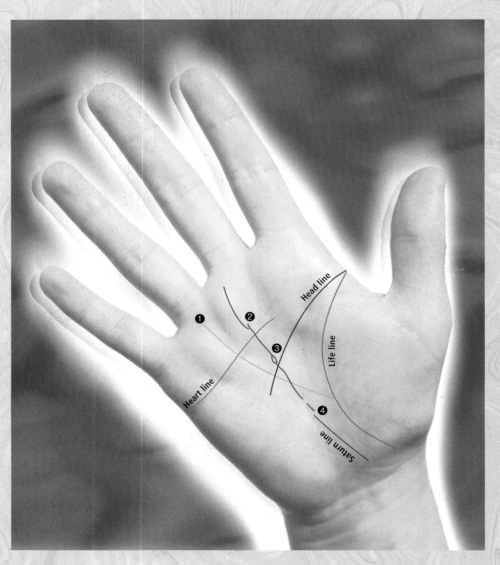

At this time a break on the Saturn line also indicates a career change ❷. This will be the key to success, because before this point the Saturn line is weak, marred by an island ❸, a little wavy and breaks that reveal gaps in employment ❹.

CHALLENGES TO REPUTATION ▶

This Saturn line indicates achievement as it runs almost straight up to the Saturn mount ❶. The Sun line is more complicated, showing a few descending lines ❷, which on the Sun line are marks reflecting temporary damage to a reputation. The break further down signifies a career change ❸.

There are a series of lines at the end of the Sun line on the Sun mount. These indicate an extremely artistic temperament and lively imagination ❹. However, so many ideas and inspirations will flow that none will be fully explored and success will be elusive. A person with these marks will have an impatient, restless character. If this is your hand, you can change this fate by focusing your efforts on one channel. If the lines on the Sun mount connect to the Sun line, each is a successful creative venture.

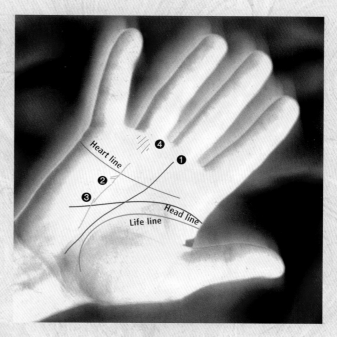

◀ ACCLAIM IN TWO FIELDS

The ascending and descending lines on the Saturn line mirror the normal ups and downs of any career ❶. The real interest on this hand is the fact that there are two Sun lines ❷, suggesting that celebrity and respect will be attained in two diverse careers. These could be writing and acting, or teaching and painting. Alternatively, if the hand is non-creative, fame would emanate from two different industries.

One of these Sun lines throws a branch to the Mercury mount ❸. Whether the branch actually reaches a mount or not, it predicts a new venture or advantageous employment in an area of work that is linked to that mount.

On this creative palm, with its sloping head line and powerful double Sun lines, the Mercury field entered could be writing or lecturing.

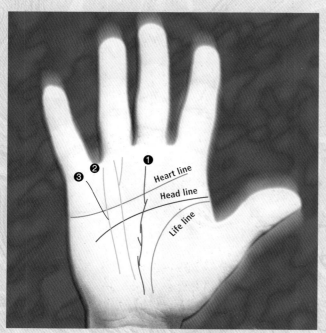

THE LADDER OF SUCCESS

It is a fortunate sign when both the Saturn and Sun lines are well marked. On this hand the Sun line also throws out two strong branches. The first of these travels to the Jupiter mount ❶, signifying that there will be an advantageous promotion or contract that gives a position of responsibility and leadership. The second branch that leaves the Sun line ends up on the Saturn mount ❷. This indicates a fresh venture or artistic enterprise connected to the qualities of the Saturn mount, which could include gardening, history, education, undertaking, watch repairing or farming. If the hand is creative this forward step could be in the field of music or possibly the clergy.

The Saturn line is unusual. It ends on the Saturn mount in what is known as the ladder of success, a rare formation ❸. A normal Saturn line runs up the hand and suddenly stops. Here, before the line stops, another short line starts, higher and further towards the Saturn mount. The second line stops, but before it does so another line

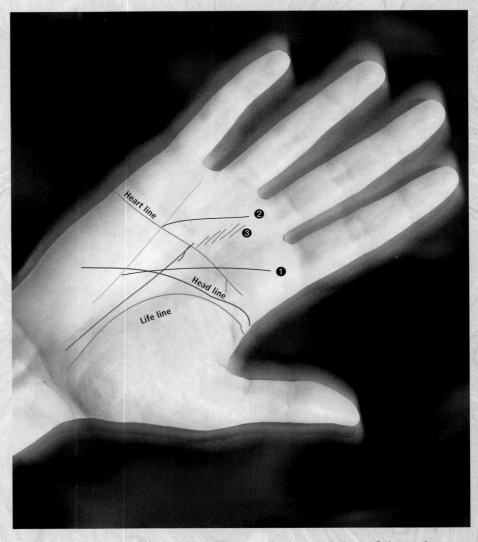

begins. There can be any number of these short lines, and, because each is nearer the thumb, they form a ladder that veers upwards to the Saturn mount. Anyone with this formation will attain success through their own efforts. The success will come in stages, each more fortunate than the last.

PROTECTION FROM SCANDAL

The Saturn line of this hand promises a good career. It also leans across towards the Sun mount, but actually ends between the Saturn finger and the Sun finger **1**. This reveals that the whole career will be biased towards creativity and the use of the imagination. Usually, success comes through an artistic role, but in other fields, innovation and originality would still be hallmarks.

The Sun line reveals a few problems. The islands early on **2** indicate a loss of face or position that lasts until the Sun line regains its normal form. The cross is a time of trouble, which will cast doubt on or reflect badly on the person's reputation **3**.
The Sun line continues strongly after the cross, suggesting that no lasting damage was caused. If the line had been weaker the person's reputation and probably their career would not have recovered. When a Sun line is stopped short of the Sun mount by an island or cross, a scandal or slander sticks and that person's career is finished.

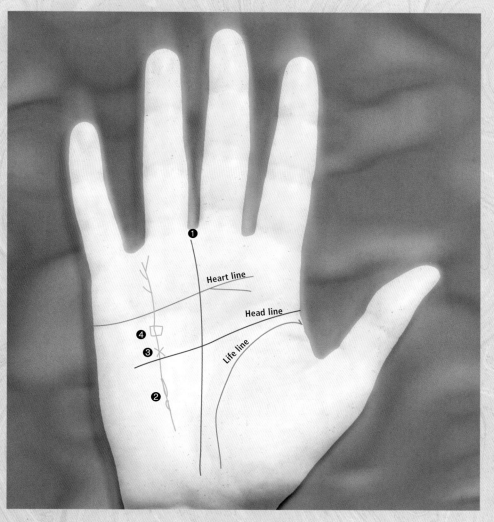

The square further along the Sun line's journey protects the person against scandal and the attempts of enemies to ruin their reputation and bring about their downfall **4**. This would take place when the person was about 45 years old. This can be assessed using the dating system from the Saturn line.

SURVIVING STRUGGLES

On this hand both the Sun ❶ and Saturn lines ❷ are marked with islands, breaks and a line of chains. Both lines are also fairly weak, a sign of struggles in life, times of unemployment and loss of money. What is interesting is that the lines keep going, so the overall picture is of financial survival despite the problems. The art in reading this hand would be to search for the reasons the career has been so challenged. Are there health troubles on the Mercury line that could affect work or outlook? Does the thumb or head line suggest a lack of willpower?

Towards the bottom of the Sun line a firm branch rises from the line and runs parallel to it for a while ❸. This indicates a second career or sideline that is actually a little better rewarded than the first. Because this happens on the Sun line and not the Saturn line, the second work path gains the individual more respect than the first.

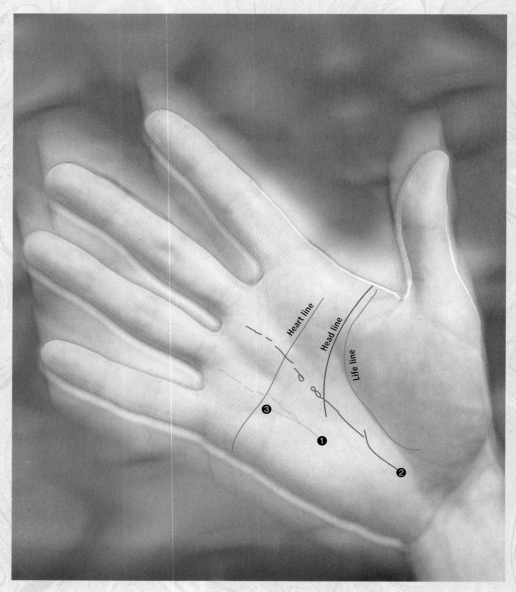

NO SATURN LINE

The most noticeable thing about this hand is that there are no real Saturn or Sun lines.

There is no need to worry if this is your hand. People without a Saturn line are often successful. They just do what they do and get on with it, without all the planning and worrying that those with Saturn lines put up with.

It used to be said that those with a Saturn line believe in, and are aware of, fate, while those without this line just accept things and never question whether there is a cosmic purpose behind it all. Eastern religions promote the doctrine of karma, the view that all events are the result of previous actions. This is true, and it is an empowering thought. Even ancient cultures, including that of Rome, with Fortuna, their goddess of fate, believed that effort and planning could improve people's lives, and that sometimes the gods would intercede to change things in response to prayer. We can mould our destinies to some extent, but we can never have absolute power over them, because the actions and decisions of other people affect us.

One negative aspect of the lack of a Sun line is that the person will have little instinctive appreciation of beauty or the arts, but life is all about evolution and this can be stimulated and learned.

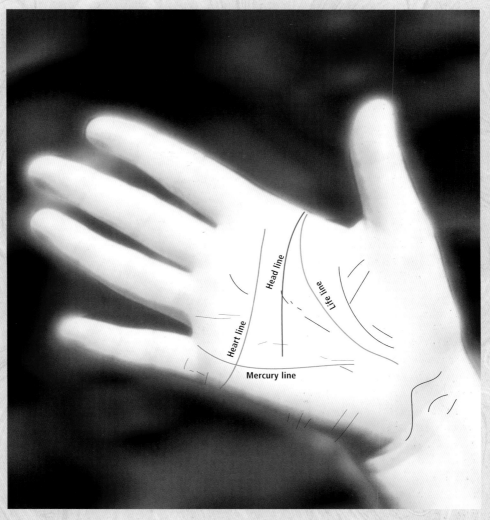

Head line

Life line

Heart line

Mercury line

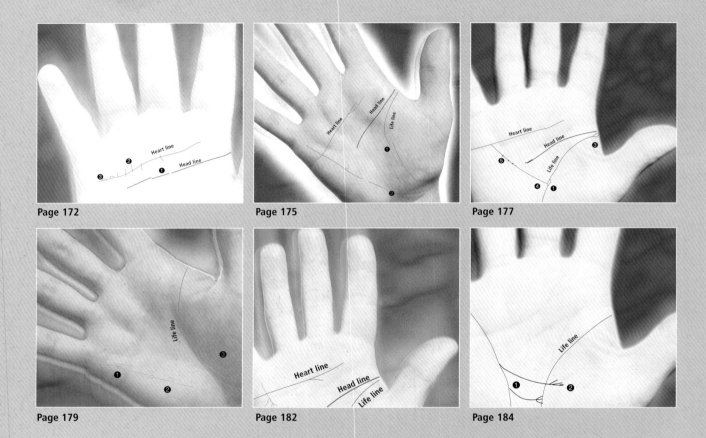

Page 172

Page 175

Page 177

Page 179

Page 182

Page 184

This chapter could pinpoint future health challenges and perhaps suggest ways in which you can keep in top shape. In more ways than one, your health is in your hands. If none of the pictures above resemble your hand, just flick through the chapter and you'll find other hands that do.

How Can I Look After My Health?

10

How can I look after my health?

Your hands are a part of you, so it makes sense that they reflect your physical and psychological wellbeing.

Your hands can reveal current health problems, physical or mental, and also point out ailments you have inherited from your parents or grandparents. Once you have pinpionted a problem or what could potentially become one, you can take appropriate steps to safeguard yourself.

When you read this chapter and discover the conditions you are prone to, do bear in mind that a lot of them, particularly problems relating to circulation, the heart and blood pressure, will usually only arise much later in life. If you are 24 years old and your nails reveal high blood pressure, don't panic; you have 25 years to get into shape.

To check health matters on the hand you should look at the condition and colour of the fingernails, as well as studying the life line, the Mercury line, the head line, the heart line, the Mars line and the Neptune plain.

The life line

• Your life line reveals the story of your health. The stronger and more uncomplicated it is, the more robust your health. The line begins under the Jupiter finger, so this portion of the line relates to early childhood, while the end of the line displays your old age. That is why the life line often grows weaker towards the wrist. A short life line does not always mean a short life, and a broken life line is not a sure omen of doom. Other lines have to be studied and, in many cases, the right and left palms examined.

Can I change the health outcome shown on my hand?

• The short answer to this question is 'yes'. The potential health problems, as well as the strength of your constitution, can be altered by changes to your lifestyle. Diet, exercise, emotional stability, a sense of fulfilment in life and, most importantly, having goals and seeking to achieve them, are all things that can enhance or impair wellbeing.
• If your palm shows a genetic predisposition to heart disease, keeping your weight in check, taking mild exercise and keeping down stress levels will ensure that the condition is far less likely to get a hold and damage you.
• It is a case of mind over matter. You will be surprised at how much better a positive attitude can make you feel. This does not mean that when you become ill, the disease is an illusion. Illness is real in the physical sense, but all ailments are exacerbated by tension and emotional pain. It is as if misery weakens the immune system, giving bacteria, viruses and the like access to your body. Be happy.

HEALTH IN THE NAILS

The fingernails are an important tool in assessing your health. They grow upwards from the finger, replacing themselves about every six months. Because they grow so fast, their colour, shape and strength mirror what is going on in your body, and they also show what ailments are embedded in your genes. It is these troubles that will arise when you enter a mature stage of life or when your system is run down through some other cause, such as stress, pregnancy or an inadequate diet.

NAIL COLOUR

The fingernails are actually clear, acting as a window on the flesh beneath.

White nails are symptomatic of anaemia. There will be a general lack of robustness, combined with a susceptibility to cold and numbness. People with white nails tire easily and feel lethargic. Remedies include additional iron and a nourishing vitamin- and mineral-rich diet. There should also be vigorous exercise to get the heart pumping, and plenty of fresh air.

Normal nails are a vital pink, slightly stronger in colour than the flesh of the fingers. The redder the nail the more robust the health. Vivid red nails indicate blood pressure, a physically passionate nature, a lack of control and a pronounced temper.

A ruddy purple colour suggests blood pressure combined with narrowing of the arteries. The darker the colour, the worse the condition.

A yellow tinge to the nails, which begins by creeping in from the edges of the nails, indicates jaundice or problems with the liver, kidney or any other internal organ that provides a cleansing role in the body. The organ has begun to fail, and

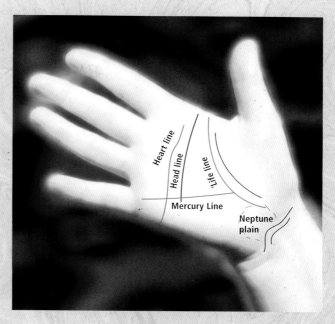

waste products are building up in the body. If the yellow colouring covers the nail the condition is acute and needs urgent attention. If the nails are bright orange an organ may be septic or undergoing severe breakdown.

A delicate blue tone speaks of recent illness, usually of the viral type or bronchitis. This colour betrays a weakened immune system and susceptibility to further illness. The prescription for this is rest, vitamin C and fresh fruit.

A stronger blue indicates poor circulation, sometimes hormonal imbalances or reproductive troubles. The colour is often seen in girls approaching puberty or women experiencing the menopause. A grey-blue around the edge of nails where they grow from the flesh is a sign that the reproductive system is under attack and should be checked. If your nails are blue just because you are cold, don't worry.

MARKS ON THE NAILS

White spots or blotches on the nails are the visible expression of inner stress and anxiety. Many tiny spots show that you are experiencing many and varied worries. A single, large mark reveals one major worry clouding your life. The fact that stress expresses itself physically in this way is proof that the problem causing it is not being handled successfully.

Time can be assessed quite accurately from the nails. A nail takes six months to grow, so a white spot halfway up a nail tells of stress three months previously. One near the base indicates a recent occurrence.

A horizontal ridge running across the nail can be anything from a faint line to what seems to be a scar left when someone tried to cut off the fingertip. Each horizontal ridge is a sign of a severe shock to the system, a serious illness or an accident trauma. The more prominent the ridge, the more pronounced the system's shock.

Ridges running vertically up the nails are an indication of lung, bronchial and throat problems, which reveals themselves as bronchitis, catarrh, asthma or allergies. The more prominent the ridges, the more troublesome the condition.

THE MOONS

The moons – the small white crescents at the base of the nails – relate to blood circulation and the heart. A normal moon covers between a fifth and a quarter of the nail's surface. Nails with no moons are a sign of an inherited propensity to high blood pressure, weakness of the heart or heart disease. When you are examining the moons, pay little attention to the ones found on the thumbs. Even if none of the fingers have moons, the thumb ones are usually present. If they are not, the blood pressure problem is serious.

Larger than normal moons are a sign of low blood pressure and are sometimes seen on athletes.

White blotches on nail

Horizontal ridges running across nail

Vertical ridges running along nail

Average moon

Small moon

No moon

Large moon

NAIL SHAPE

Long nails, which curve like talons, suggest troubles with the spine and back pain. Short, broad nails, which seem bulbous because they are curved, may indicate tuberculosis or tubercular illness. If the nails are blue, the condition is worse, with an increased susceptibility to pneumonia.

A square end to the nail is a sign of blood pressure. People with narrow nails have weaker constitutions and are more prone to illness, a characteristic that is even more pronounced in people with small nails.

Nails that are sunk into the flesh mirror an anxious nature, neuroses and illnesses related to the nervous system, as do brittle nails that curving out at the edges. These also reveal a general debility.

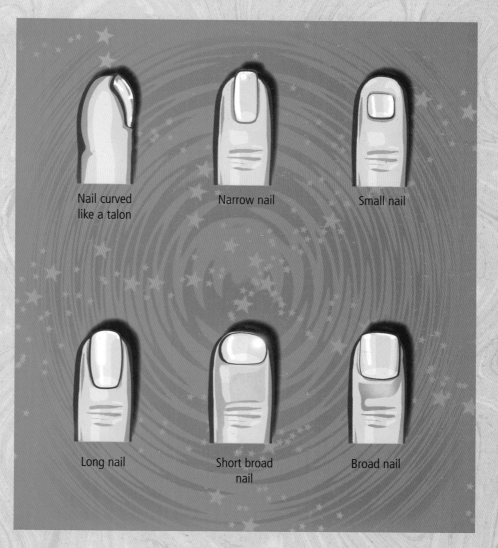

Nail curved like a talon

Narrow nail

Small nail

Long nail

Short broad nail

Broad nail

Dry-looking nails are a sign that necessary oils are missing from the diet. Cod liver oil or olive oil taken internally will help overcome the problem.

People with long nails suffer most from ailments afflicting the upper half of the body: the head, back, chest, neck, throat and lungs. If the nails are long and curved, conditions affecting the lung and throat will be to the fore. People with short nails have more difficulty with the lower half of their bodies: the heart, digestive and reproductive systems, hips, legs and feet.

MENTAL ILLNESS

The head line is affected by several tiny breaks **❶**. Each one tells of a temporary period when the mind was unable to function properly, which could be the result of physical injury to the head or brain, a birth defect or a mental illness. It is possible that a prolonged period of taking mind-altering medication could produce these lines. They sometimes appear on the hands of people addicted to hard drugs whose powers of rational thought have been badly damaged.

If the break in a head line is severe it can mean an extended period when the person is unable to lead a normal life.

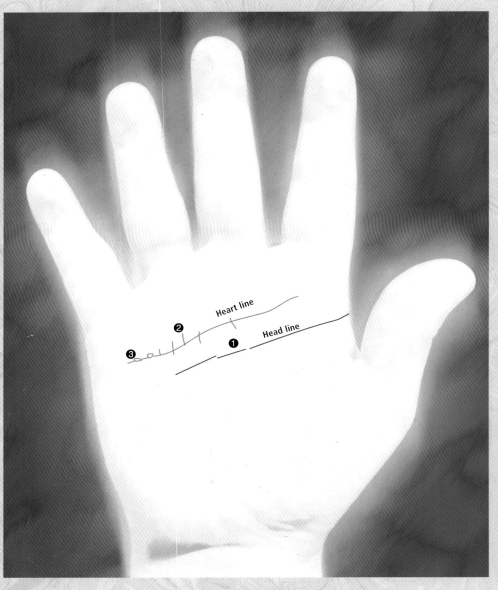

Heart line

Head line

The bars that cut the heart line can be read as disappointments in love **❷**, but they are also signs of weakness of the heart or liver. Often, when the liver is not functioning at its peak, the heart line will take on a yellowish tinge. The tiny circles on the heart line are also warnings of heart trouble **❸**.

HEAD ACHES

This head line is marked by tiny hair lines, some ascending, others descending ❶. These are associated with headaches or migraines or with any head pain that is severe enough to affect a person's ability to function. This does not mean a normal life will be impossible but that certain days will be lost from work because of this problem.

The islands can relate to headaches, but they generally symbolize phases of mental weakness or an inability to focus, sometimes caused by migraine or headache problems ❷.

The dots on the heart line show a tendency towards palpitations. Someone who has these dots is often emotional and prone to anxiety. If the dots are black or bluish they can indicate malaria, rheumatic fever and other extreme heat-producing illnesses ❸.

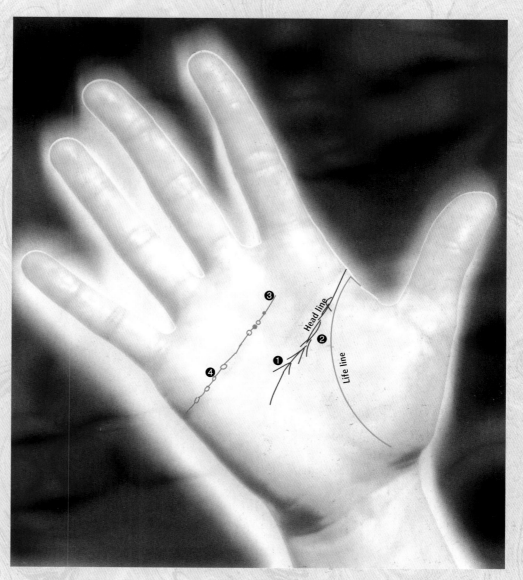

The circles are a greater cause for concern because they suggest heart troubles ❹. If this is your hand, make sure you eat healthy, pure foods and take time out to relax.

BLUE PERIODS

The long head line on this hand slopes downwards ❶. This is a sign of a vibrantly creative imagination and of a romantic spirit that is unworldly and impractical. From the point of view of health, however, it's a marker for depression. Not clinical depression, but blue periods of despair. The more the head line slopes and the further it travels towards the wrist, the greater the problem will be.

The life line has become a chain in two places ❷. Where each piece of chain marks the life line the person will be troubled by ill-health. The chains do not indicate the exact type of illness, but it can normally be divined by searching elsewhere on the hand. For example, the first section of chaining is at the beginning of the life line, under the Jupiter mount, which is a sign of ill-health in early life. As usual, all events or periods on the life line can be dated using the line's own dating system.

The circles on the heart line are omens of heart trouble ❸ Here, they are well defined, and the larger they are, the more severe the difficulties

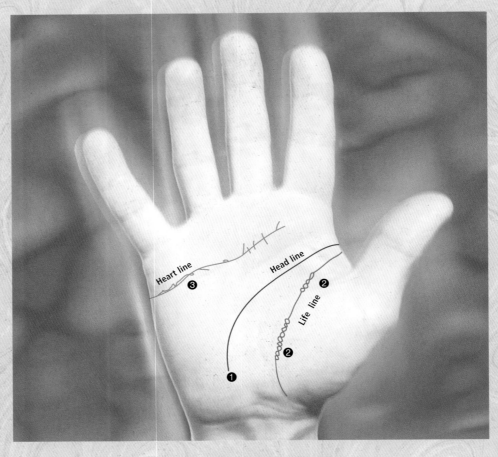

Heart line ❸   Head line ❷   Life line ❷ ❷   ❶

they bring. This link between signs on the heart line and certain ailments as well as emotional or mental states puzzles many people. It seems, for example, to suggest that everyone with dots on the heart line is unlucky in love as well as suffering from heart palpitations. The truth is that we are composite creatures, consisting of soul, mind and body. Mental and emotional states can trigger illness, while ill-health can cause depression, which in turn can have a direct impact on relationships.

A SERIOUS ILLNESS

There is a clearly marked break in the life line at around the age of 29 ❶, revealing an onslaught by a serious illness at the time. If the break is shown on one hand only, the patient will recover.

This hand has a Mercury line running up the hand to the Mercury mount ❷. It is a little wavy and fairly weak, showing a rather weak constitution and regular fluctuations in health. This is also a sign of a disposition that is inclined to worry, something that never encourages good health.

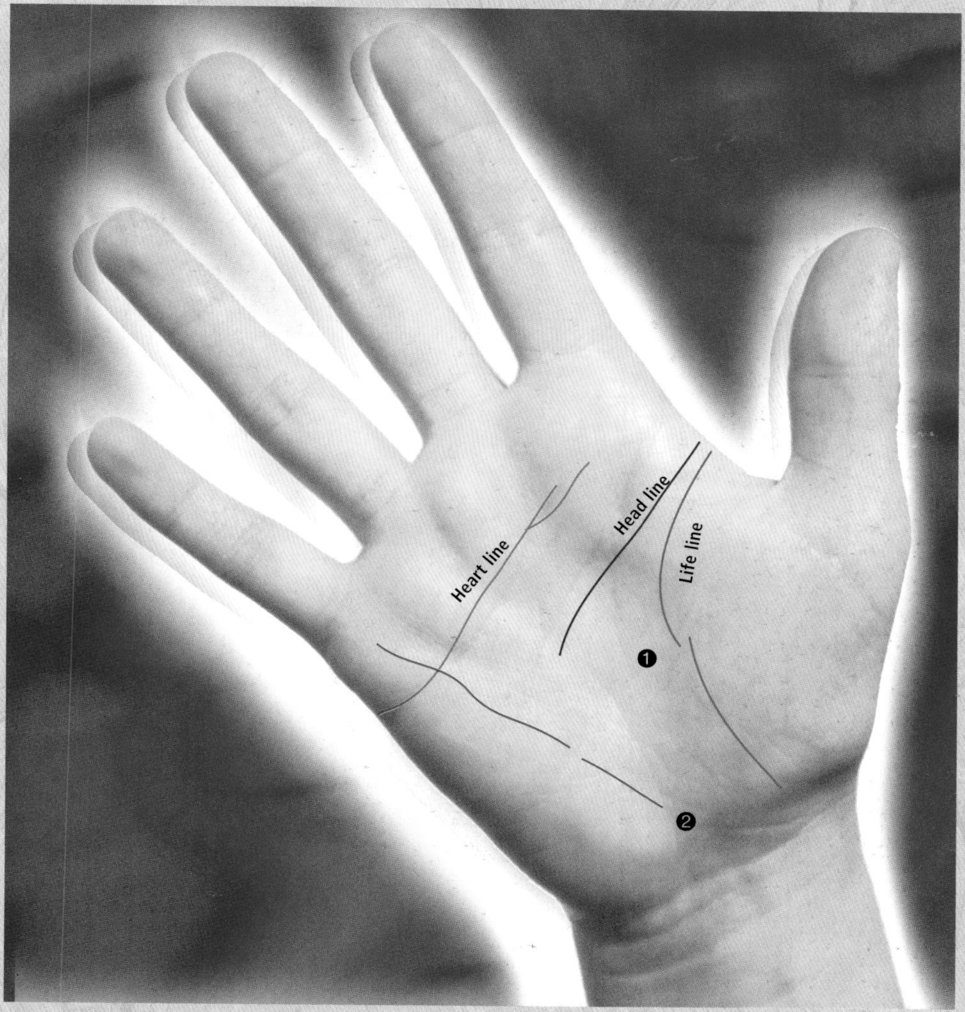

The Mercury line is sometimes known as the health line, and in earlier times it was called the hepatica or liver line, because it was believed that the health of that organ could be diagnosed from it. The line is an indicator of mental states as well as general wellbeing and a person's predisposition to certain ailments. It also relates to business acumen and career prospects.

Heart line

Head line

Life line

GOOD HEALTH

On this hand the Mercury line is noticeable by its absence. When it is missing completely, the person's health is generally good. The reasoning behind this is that because the line reveals illnesses, when it's not there, most of the health troubles are missing, too. However, an absent Mercury line is a sign of digestive difficulties and frequent sharp headaches.

There are many hair lines falling from the life line and clinging to it ❶. These tiny lines bring weakness, loss of vitality and susceptibility to infection. The parts of the life line that are clear of them will be blessed by better health. Work out when and how long it is before the health recovers (see page 89) and by checking the date on the life line itself.

The life line also end in a number of hair lines. This is normal, displaying a general weakening of the body's function before death in old age.

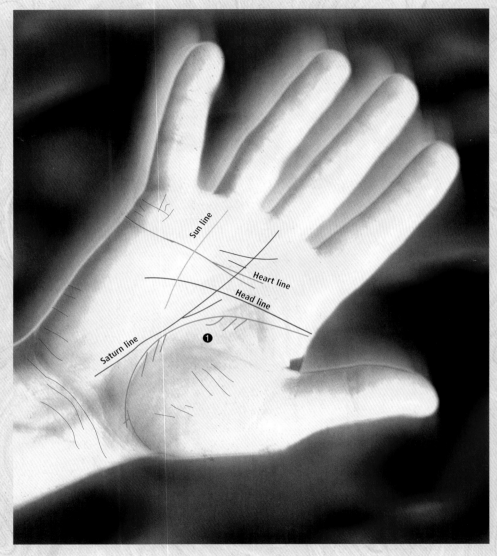

Sun line

Heart line

Head line

Saturn line

❶

HEART DISEASE

There are three islands marked on the life line of this hand. The second ❶ and third islands ❷ symbolize an illness or a loss of wellbeing. The bad patch will continue as long as the island, and the age when it begins and later ends can be divined from the life line.

The first island is an exception to the rule. Any island at the start of the life line under the Jupiter mount indicates that there is a mystery surrounding the birth.❸ This is found on the hands of people who were adopted or who were misled about the identity of their parents. It was, for example, common in the 20th century for a single young woman who gave birth to pass her child off as the offspring of her parents.

The Mercury line runs from the heart line to the life line ❹, warning of weakness and disease of the heart. If the Mercury line is pale in colour and rather broad, the heart's action will be poor and the circulation bad; if it is red, it is a sign of active heart disease.

There are also tiny dots on the Mercury line ❺, as if someone had pressed a ball-point pen into the flesh. These signify attacks by virus, but there is no need to panic if you have these marks on

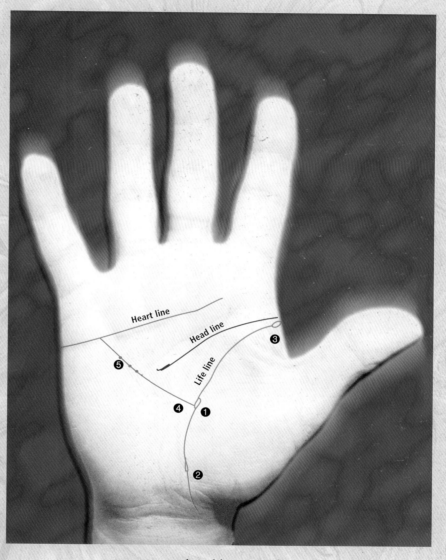

your own hand because the common cold and influenza are caused by viruses. Red dots show a health problem that will cause fever, and if there are several they indicate a tendency to run temperatures.

PRESERVATION ▶

A strong Mercury line slopes gently in towards the palm's centre ❶. The more powerful the Mercury line, the stronger the health. It is a positive sign when the line stays near the Moon mount. The closer it gets to the life line, the more health problems there will be. Often, the Mercury line nears the life line as they descend the palm, showing a natural weakening of the constitution with age.

There are two squares on the life line. When the life line runs through a square it indicates protection from an incident, operation or accident that could have led to death ❷.

The second square has an island within it, indicating that it is a sign of preservation from illness ❸. It signifies that any illness will not cause lasting harm.

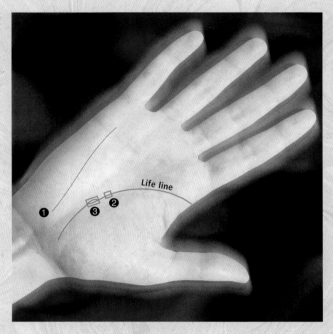

◀CHEST COMPLAINTS

A Mercury line that is formed of, or marked by, many little islands reveals asthmatic and bronchial complaints ❶. Larger islands relate to serious respiratory diseases, such as tuberculosis and emphysema. If the Mercury line is free of these islands for any length, there will be periods of life that will be free of these problems.

The life line on this hand is rather weak and lies close to the Venus mount ❷. The weaker the life line and the nearer it runs to the Venus mount, the less robust the constitution.

There are two squares on the life line. The first covers a break in the life line and is a sign of protection from a sudden life-threatening event ❸. The second has a short line running from it that ends on the Mars plain. This square preserves the person from an accident ❹.

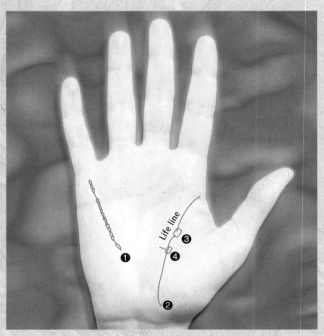

NEUROSIS

This Mercury line has one or two tiny islands **❶**, indicating that there may be some asthma or a proneness to coughs and chest infections. The main problem is that the line is formed of a series of tiny lines rather than one strong one **❷**. This affects the person's mental health, suggesting that they will have a neurotic character with a tendency to worry and, perhaps, problems when it comes to processing information logically. In extreme cases, it can be a sign of paranoia, schizophrenia or depression.

Physically, this type of configuration warns of problems with the digestive system and the waste-processing organs, such as the liver or bladder. The Mercury line would have a yellowish tone if the liver or bladder were strongly affected.

If this is your hand meditate to create inner harmony and stick to a pure diet as far as you can.

The life line is a little close to the Venus mount, which indicates a weakening of the overall constitution **❸**.

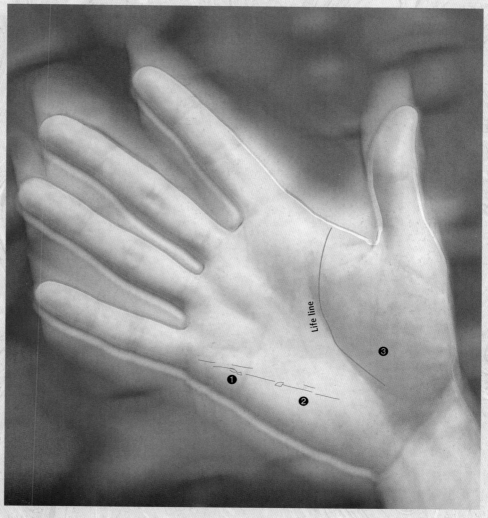

CREAKY JOINTS ▶

This Mercury line snakes down the palm and has fine lines ascending from it ❶. A wavy Mercury line points to health problems associated with rheumatism, arthritis and gout or fever-based illnesses, such as malaria or influenza, which will adversely affect the career.

The fine ascending lines are fortunate marks ❷. Each one indicates a period of better health and increased vitality.

The life line is powerful and curves out into the hand, far from the Venus mount. This signifies a basically robust constitution and lots of energy ❸. This would be complicated by the wavy Mercury line, but the fine ascending lines will help to make sure that the life is not too severely affected by any health problems.

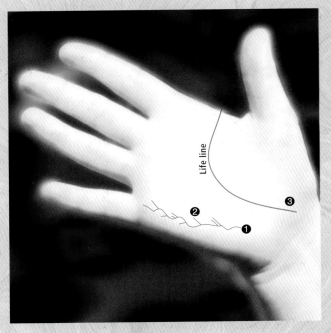

◀DIGESTIVE ORDERS

The life line is weak and hugs the Venus mount, suggesting a lack of vibrancy and energy ❶.

The Mercury line is twisted ❷, indicating a highly strung nature and warning of liver troubles and stomach conditions, possibly stomach ulcers or malfunction of the gall bladder or pancreas.

On some hands the Mercury line is twisted for only part of its length. In these cases the problems occur for a while and then clear up. To date ailments on the Mercury line, imagine a straight line running across the palm to the life line. What age does the life line give for the point your imaginary line crosses it?

The fine descending lines from the Mercury mount suggest the owner will be troubled by minor health irritations, such as recurrent sore throats, skin rashes or digestive upsets ❸.

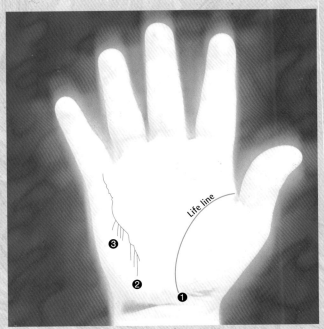

A WEAK HEAD

The Mercury line starts from the head line and runs across to the life line, revealing a weakness or infection affecting the head or brain 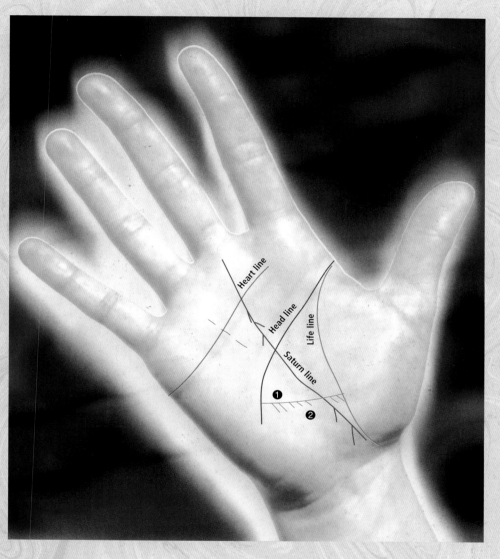. If the life line carries on as normal beyond the point at which this type of Mercury line touches it, the difficulty is not serious enough to change the life completely or to affect the physical health. If the life line is weaker or is marked with chains or islands after the Mercury line reaches it, the quality of life or at least the lifestyle will be affected by the ailment. The point at which the Mercury line reaches the life line can reveal the age at which this affliction begins.

There are also some fine lines descending from the Mercury line, showing other minor health worries ❷.

A CHALLENGE ▶

This strong Mercury line promises a generally good level of health. There is, however, a break in it, which is preceded by a few tiny descending lines, which indicate minor health irritations ❶. A break in the Mercury line symbolizes an illness that challenges the system ❷. Fortunately, on this hand a second Mercury line begins before the first one ends. However, because a break always indicates a severe problem, it's likely that it could lead to changes in this person's attitudes and lifestyle.

Further down the Mercury line a line branches out and travels to the life line ❸. This signifies an event that affects the health but not in a serious way. This problem can be dated from the point the branch line from the Mercury mount reaches the life line. Here, it is at the ages of 39 or 40.

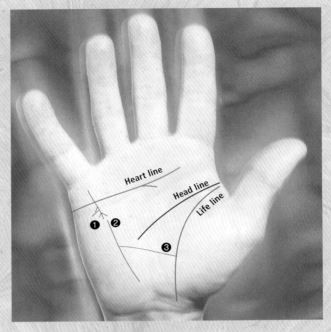

◀ NORMAL SERVICE RESUMED

This Mercury line shows a clean break, with a clear gap between the end of the line and its beginning further up the hand ❶. This type of break suggests that will be a period of illness during which normal life, work and activities are put on hold until the Mercury line begins again. The gap shown here is quite short, indicating an illness lasting for two or three years.

Below the break a strong line branches out from the Mercury line and runs across the hand, cuts the life line and ends on the Venus mount ❷. When a line from the Mercury mount cuts the life line rather than being stopped by it, expect a health problem that will affect the way you lead your life and something that you will have to adjust to.

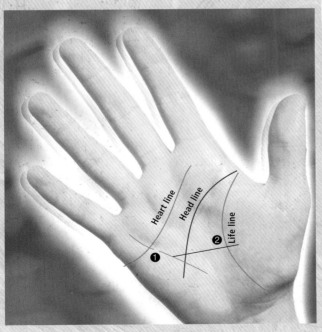

PERILS OF OLD AGE

The Mercury line illustrated on this hand splits into three forks just before it ends near the wrist ❶. This is a sign that the body's strength will fade in old age. The more forks there are, the frailer the body will become. Also, the higher up the Mercury line the forks begin, the earlier the constitution and physical strength will being to fade. On this hand the three forks are right at the Mercury line's end, so weakening will occur in old age, at the end of the life. This reading is confirmed by a similar forking at the end of the life line ❷.

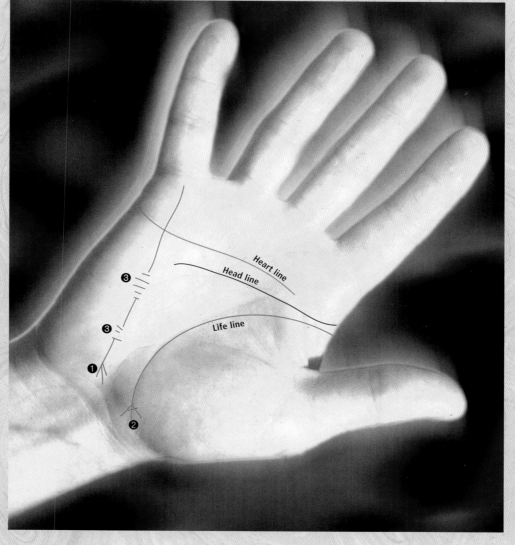

Heart line
Head line
Life line

At two points on the Mercury line there are a series of horizontal lines ❸. Each time these lines appear points to severe problems with the liver or another processing organ, sometimes the gall bladder, pancreas or kidney. When an illness is represented by this formation, it indicates that the resulting health problems will cause a desperate struggle with money, employment or business. Because this Mercury line shows two groups of horizontal lines, there will be two period when illness of this kind will strike.

SHORTAGE OF BREATH

This hand shows two lines branching away from the Mercury line and travelling across the palm to the life line, where they both end in a number of forks. Some of these forked lines cross the life line, others do not. Whereas a single line touching the life line points to a significant ailment, it is always one that fails to affect a person's lifestyle in any real way ❶, while a line that crosses the life line presages a health problem that does affect the way life is lived ❷.

In this case, each line that runs across or to the life line pinpoints a separate health concern that either compromises everyday life or is more easily coped with. Since the smaller lines are produced by branches running from the Mercury mount, they are complications arising from the original illness or lesser ailments that have developed only because the constitution had been weakened by the original problem. The Mercury line runs down the

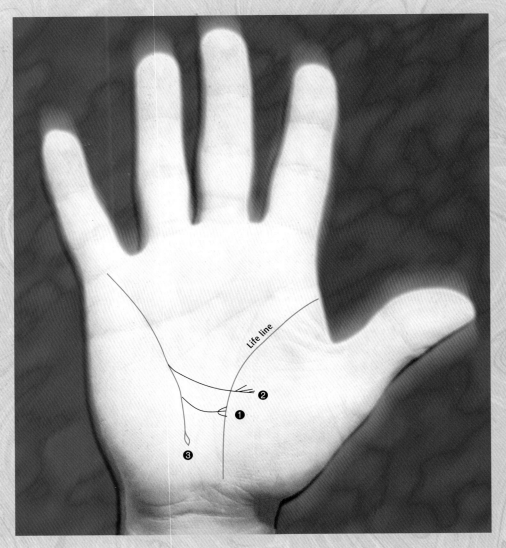

Life line

hand and finishes in a large island ❸. This foretells a period of respiratory difficulties at the life's end. There is no ultimate recovery from these, and it is likely that death is caused or hastened by breathing difficulties.

ORGAN TROUBLE

The Mercury line on this hand has three strong bars across it **❶**. Each bar symbolizes the onset of an illness that temporarily halts progress through life. This would normally be associated with the liver, kidneys, gall bladder or pancreas and sometimes the spleen.

The Mercury line runs across the hand and ends at the life line **❷**. It is noticeable that at this point the life line is stronger than the Mercury line. This indicates that there will be a serious problem, such as an operation or debilitating illness, but because the life line is more robust than the Mercury line, the crisis is overcome and life goes on.

If you can manage to look at lots of different hands you will become aware that it is rare for the Mercury line to meet the life line further up the hand (nearer the fingers). This would signify a major health problem early in life. Most Mercury-life line meetings mean an illness or health problem in later life, which is perfectly natural. Most of us can expect at least one serious health battle as we age and youth's strength fades.

The age at which this takes place can be divined by the life line's own dating system.

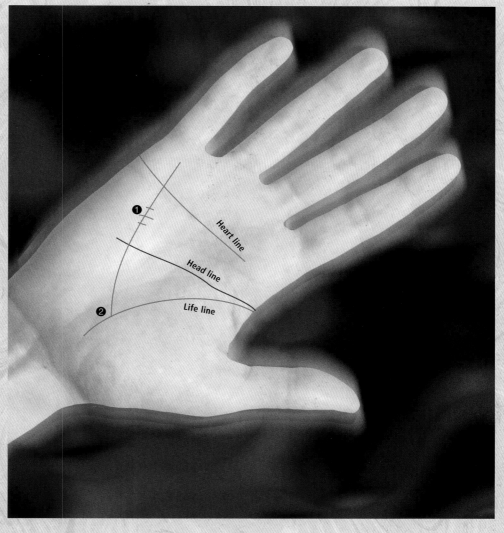

Heart line

Head line

Life line

CHILDHOOD AILMENTS

At the beginning of the Mercury line on the Mercury mount the line is made up of a few tiny lines ❶. This shows a few childhood ailments or perhaps a general weakness early in life. The Mercury line regains its strength as it runs down the hand, so these early health difficulties clear up quickly.

The Mercury line runs down the palm and crosses the life line. At the point that the lines cross, the Mercury line is the more powerful ❷. In the past, palmists believed this was a sign of taking passage to the next world, resulting from an illness or the failure of some organ. At the least, it is a major challenge to the system. The age at which this crisis takes place should be judged from the life line.

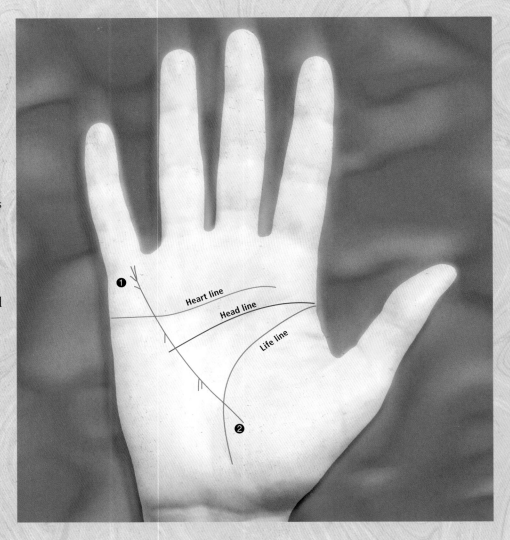

This type of configuration raises the question: 'Can I do anything to extend life and health?' The best advice is to eat well and healthily, to exercise and above all to keep the mind calm, content and positive. People who enjoy life, live longer. It has also been noted that those who have something to live for, a purpose in their lives, live longer. This aim can be creativity, a love of writing or painting, spirituality, good company, travel and gardening, or a responsibility in caring for a loved companion, animal or bird.

STOMACH CONDITIONS

The Mercury line illustrated here is twisted and complicated by the lines that are wrapped around it **❶**. This is similar to a chain formation, and it signifies digestive problems and discomfort associated with eating. This pinpoints the area of the problems but not their cause, which could range from a stomach ulcer to a twisted colon or hiatus hernia. There could also be difficulties with the bladder or glands, such as the thyroid. Mentally, these symptoms could cause a general lack of concentration, which would hinder the career and dull ambition.

Fortunately, the Mercury line clears up and becomes normal lower down the hand, indicating that these ailments disappear in later life **❷**. This could be a natural change, the result of a breakthrough in medical science or just a complete transformation in the person's lifestyle.

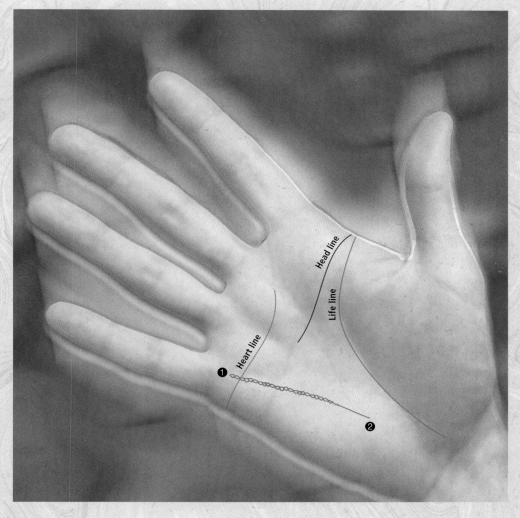

Head line

Life line

Heart line

GYNAECOLOGICAL PROBLEMS

What is immediately noticeable about the palm that is illustrated here is that there are two Mercury lines ❶. Because a Mercury line suggests that the person has a propensity towards a health problem of one kind or another, two Mercury lines indicate that there are two, simultaneous illnesses or health-related problems. The nature of each Mercury line needs to be studied to determine what ailments predominate. Are they broken or are there chains or islands?

Usually when there are two Mercury lines, one is shorter or weaker than the other, indicating that one illness will last longer and affect the person's life more seriously.

A robust Mars line curves round the outer edge of the Venus mount, following the path of the life line ❷. This is an excellent health line, granting vitality and a sound constitution. On this hand it would indicate that the health problems represented by the dual Mercury lines and Neptune plain ❸ would not be able to adversely affect the person's general wellbeing.

There are a number of fine lines and a grille

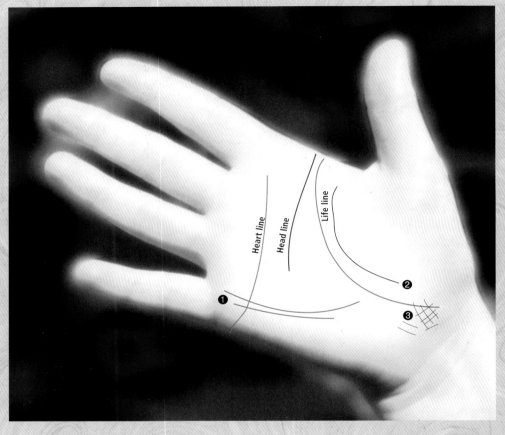

marking the Neptune plain, and these signify that gynaecological problems will be an on-and-off, but fairly constant problem throughout life. They can also suggest a highly strung, emotional nature, which can lead to a string of unsatisfactory relationships or affairs and sometimes even obsessions with partners. Do bear in mind that it is ludicrous to say that all people with gynaecological problems have unsatisfactory love lives. Confirmation of this would have to be searched for elsewhere on the hand. Look at the heart line and Venus mount for clues.

TROUBLE REPRODUCING

The life line of this hand reveals health difficulties in the form of a few little breaks and in its general weakness ❶. Fortunately, a strong Mars line follows it down the hand and makes up for the lack of strength in the health lines, by granting extra physical energy and protection from the health troubles shown on the life line ❷.

With practice, it is easy to tell the difference between a Mars line and any influence line that shadows the life line on the Venus mount. The Mars line is always much stronger than any influence line.

There are two lines running into the Neptune plain from below the bracelets ❸. The first bracelet also arches up from the wrist on to the plain ❹. Both these marks suggest serious problems with reproductive organs. They may not necessarily indicate sterility, but they are certainly worrying enough to require medical attention as soon as they are noticed.

These formations can also be signs of deep-rooted emotional or sexual hang-ups, resulting from childhood trauma, a deeply unsettling divorce or gender-orientation problems.

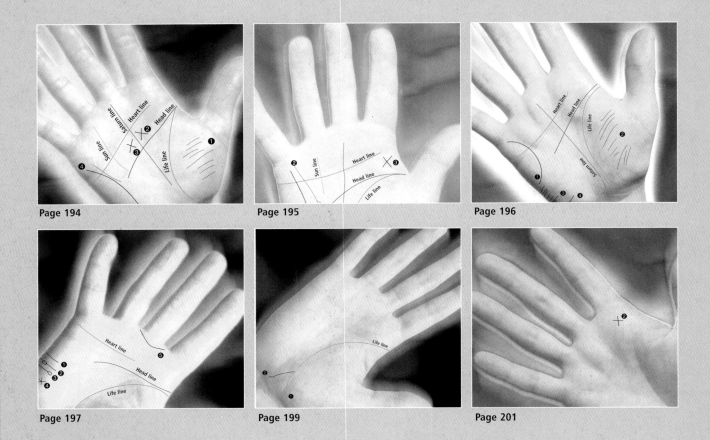

Page 194

Page 195

Page 196

Page 197

Page 199

Page 201

This chapter could explain about any odd markings you've noticed on your hand. The crosses, circles, stars etc, that you've always wondered about. We are all individuals, so we all have something special on our hands. As you look through the next few pages you might find a mark or two, that is mirrored on your hand.

Is There Anything Special About My Hand?

11

Is There Anything Special About My Hand?

All hands are special. No two are alike, and many palms also have markings on them that are rare or that do not quite fit under the broad headings of emotional life, career or anything else.

Some of these marks will be described and discussed in this chapter. Have a good look at the thumbnail sketches to see if any of the markings or lines shown appear on your own hands. You might be lucky and discover something interesting about yourself.

Look out for palm symbols such as stars, triangles, squares, islands and circles, a few travel lines or perhaps an intuition line. Happy hunting.

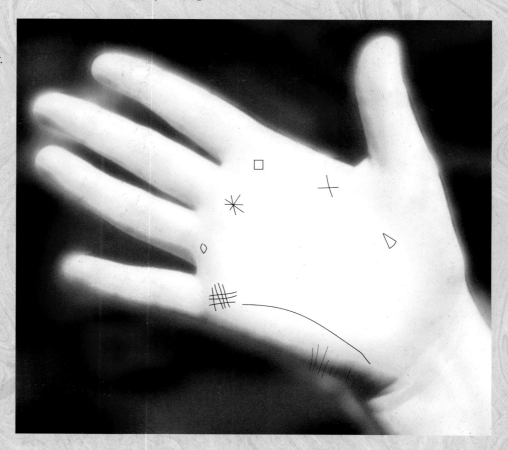

MYSTICAL CROSSES

The many fine lines shown running across the Venus mount towards the life line are known as sensitivity or worry lines ❶. Most palms have ten or more, while others have over a hundred. When there are more than about 15 they indicate a sensitive nature, which is given to worrying. If, as in the illustration, the Venus mount is packed with them, they suggest a highly strung, sometimes oversensitive worrier, who can be obsessive and who often worries about nothing. It is, however, unusual to find a hand with no sensitivity lines.

The crosses marked between the heart and head lines are mystical crosses ❷ and ❸. These crosses work on three levels – material, intellectual and spiritual – and when they are firmly marked on a hand that displays intuition, steadiness, strength of will and intelligence they indicate that the person has a fascination with psychic development, magic and the mysteries of life.

If they are found on the hand of a fidgety, nervous person, there will be a greater inclination towards wanting to know what everyone else is up to and the tendency to pass on information. These people love to know the end of everything, and they analyse too much.

On a practical, scientific hand a mystical cross displays extreme intellectual curiosity, love of research, study, exploration and experimentation. This urge to understand leads logically to religion or spirituality, which can provide the ultimate answers.

Everyone with a mystical cross shares attributes. The gossip will be interested in psychic subjects; the researcher will be drawn to astrology;

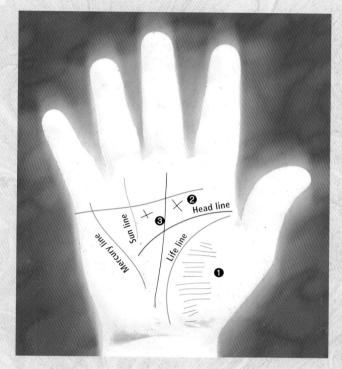

and the mystic will still love to know what their neighbours are doing. All have spiritual potential.

When it is well marked and not joined to other lines, a mystical cross reveals a powerful mind, which delves into the mysteries seriously but often keeps that part of their life hidden or shares it only with select associates. The knowledge and beliefs gathered will affect their perceptions, attitudes and actions. The career is mainly kept quite separate, because the person usually prefers not to mix spiritual studies with worldly activities.

When there are two or more mystical crosses, the effect is emphasized.

The four-armed cross is an age-old religious symbol, often used to denote the ultimate deity.

INTUITION

This hand has several deep sensitivity lines on the Venus mount within the life line ❶. When there are only a few of these lines the person worries only when there is a real problem or uncertainty about their own life or that of someone they care for or about the nation or world.

These lines are easy to distinguish from the influence lines that cross the Venus mount and either touch the life line or cross it. Influence lines are obviously stronger, and often do not begin as far towards the thumb as sensitivity lines.

Between the head and heart lines are two mystical crosses. One of them is below the Saturn mount ❷, which indicates an intellect that is drawn to magic and mysticism. This is a sign of someone who wishes to pierce the veils and experience the secrets of the universe; someone who is willing to get involved in meditation or other spiritual or occult practices, and to take charge of their own fate and spiritual development. When this type of mystical cross is strong, with a pronounced intuition lines, it augurs success in magical or psychic studies.

The other mystical cross is actually formed from the Saturn line ❸. This indicates that the career will be influenced or even formed by the person's spiritual beliefs. This can be within an orthodox religious establishment or an alternative spirituality.

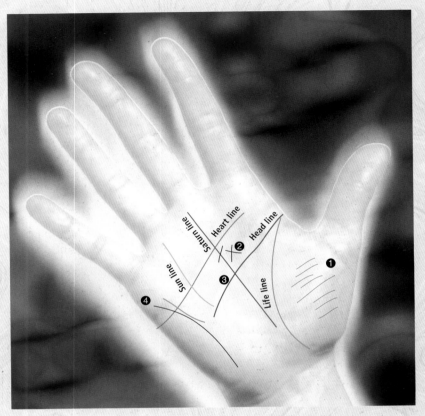

It used to be thought that a mystical cross touching the Saturn line and positioned below the Saturn mount predicted a flourishing career in the church or other religious organization.

The hand does have a prominent intuition line ❹. This describes a crescent, which runs from the Mercury mount to the Moon mount. This formation provides an excellent sense of intuition, inspiration that guides, sometimes manifesting as infallible instincts, and sometimes as the gift of prophecy. On this hand the intuitive, psychic sense will blend with the mystical interests to give insight and wisdom.

SENSITIVITY

A strong line of intuition can be clearly seen arcing from the Mercury mount to the base of the Moon mount ❶. It is easy to distinguish the line of intuition from the Mercury line. There is a Mercury line on this hand, but the intuition line begins on the Mercury mount and always ends on the Moon mount, while the Mercury line begins on the Mercury mount and moves diagonally across the hand towards the life line and Venus mount ❷.

The intuition line reveals a deep sense of intuition, sensitivity to the atmosphere of places, the emotions of others, sometimes previous events about an area or individual and even glimpses of future happenings. Such knowledge comes as inspiration and is not controllable, except that these 'knowings' can be listened to or ignored. A powerful intuition line will bring vivid dreams, even precognitive ones.

The mystical cross is positioned under the Jupiter mount ❸, where it suggests someone with an inquiring mind but who will explore knowledge only when it relates to their own lives or when it could be of interest or use to themselves. They will explore any avenues that help them mark out their own fate or optimum career path, and it has been noticed that people with this type of mystical cross are eager to consult clairvoyants and astrologers to divine their future.

For those with this mark, the life path can lead to inner searching and spiritual growth.

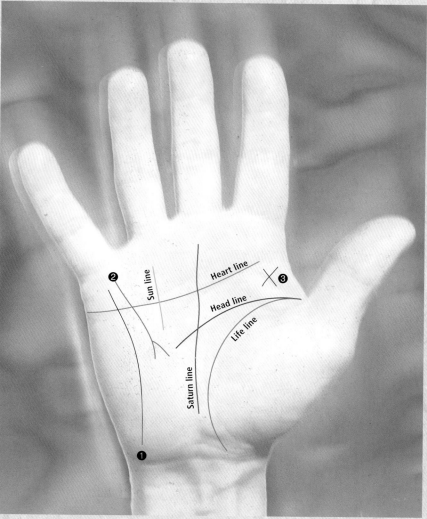

TRAVELS IN THE MIND

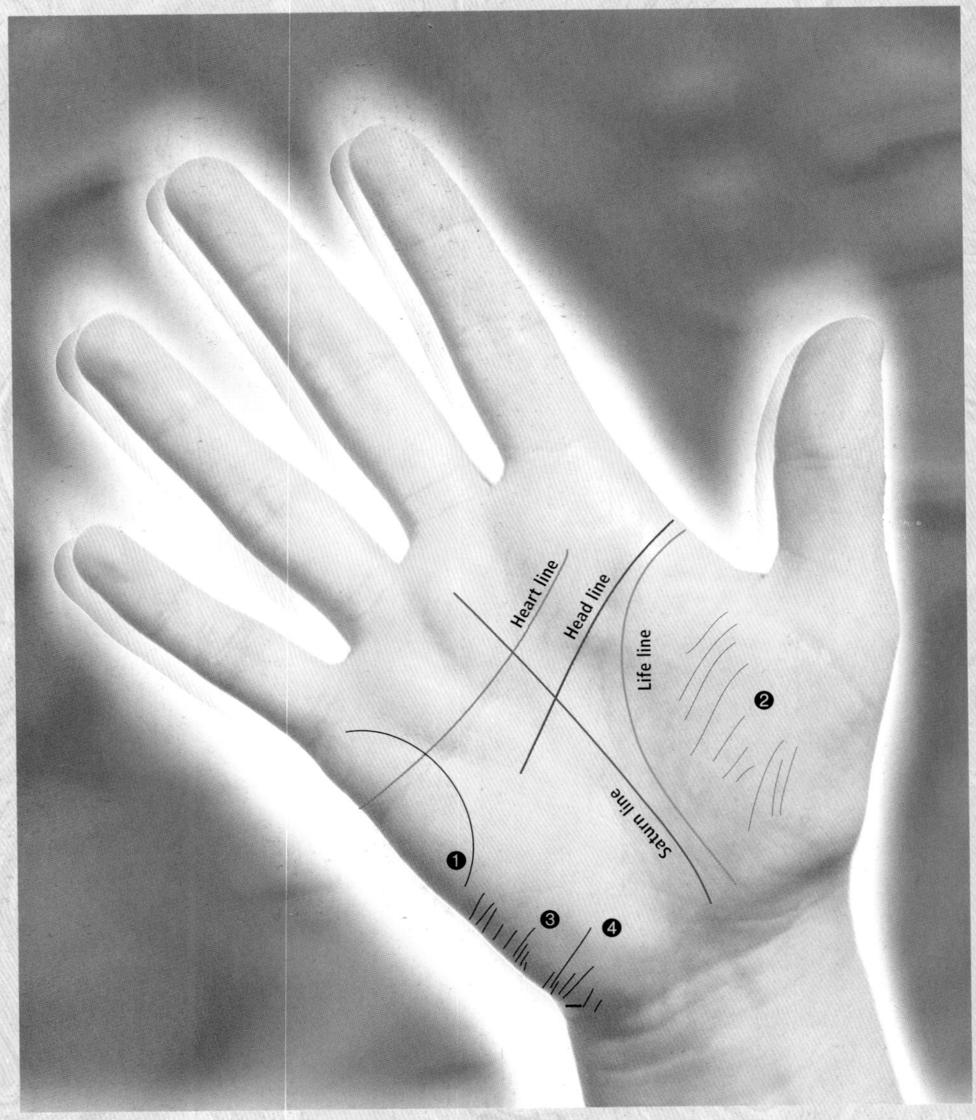

On this hand the intuition line almost takes the form of a semicircle, beginning on the Mercury mount and circling round to the top of the Moon mount ❶. Such a line is an indicator of a strong sense of intuition, but it is combined with an introverted nature. The intuitions will be inward looking and even when they do relate to the outside world, they will often be kept private. This type of intuition line will often appear along with other signs of a sensitive nature, and this particular hand shows many sensitivity lines on the Venus mount within the life line ❷.

The fine lines on the Moon mount at the hand's edge are all travel lines ❸. Travel lines can either relate to physical journeys, holidays or explorations overseas or to journeys that take place within the mind, to fantasy realms and oceans. The travels are imaginary when the travel lines are fine and there are many of them, as in the hand shown, which is also a sensitive hand. However, there are one or two stronger travel lines, and these are probably signs of real journeys ❹.

Heart line

Head line

Life line

Saturn line

TRAVELS IN THE WORLD

The travel lines on this hand are well marked, indicating that they represent physical journeys to other countries. Some are longer than others ❶. Logically, the lengthier travel lines indicate journeys of greater length and duration. Travel means different things to different people, but usually a longer line would show a six-month holiday backpacking around Australia, while a small one could be a weekend in Paris.

One travel line has a square on it ❷. This indicates the presence of danger on a journey but reassures that it will end safely with no lasting damage done.

Another ends in an island ❸, which tells of a loss during a journey, which could be the loss of money, of a prized personal possession or even the end of a friendship.

One travel line finishes in a cross, which is a sign of a disappointing or unsuccessful trip ❹.

Because there are so many challenging travel lines, it can be assumed that the owner of this hand enjoys more adventurous journeys, perhaps exploring dangerous terrain or less well-known places.

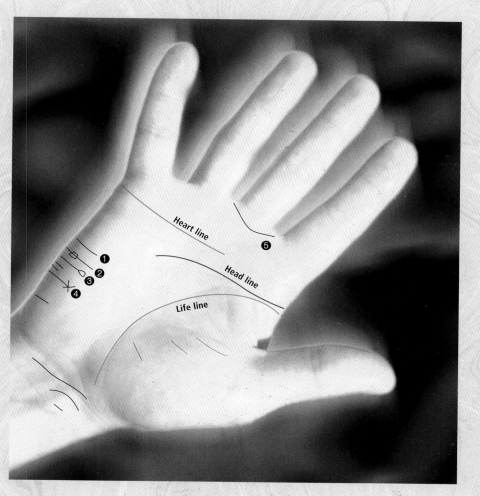

The semicircular line running around the base of the Saturn finger is the Saturn ring ❺, a mark that hinders success in life, and shows someone who is full of big ideas and plans but who always gives up and leaves projects uncompleted. It generally means that ambitions will not be fulfilled, but always because the temperament causes a lack of continuity. If this is your hand, commit yourself to one path to overcome these problems.

SIGNIFICANT JOURNEYS

On this hand are two travel lines that extend into the palm and reach the Saturn line ❶. These represent significant journeys, each of which will be of great length and which will have a profound effect on the person, altering their attitudes and perceptions and influencing or even changing their career.

The travel line that droops down towards the wrist reveals a less successful excursion ❷, an unfortunate, loss-making adventure or a financially ruinous trip.

The travel line with chains and the broken line signify that delays, obstacles and misfortunes occurred during the journey ❸.

The circle on the Moon mount is traditionally believed to warn of a danger of drowning. If this is on your hand, rule out wind surfing ❹.

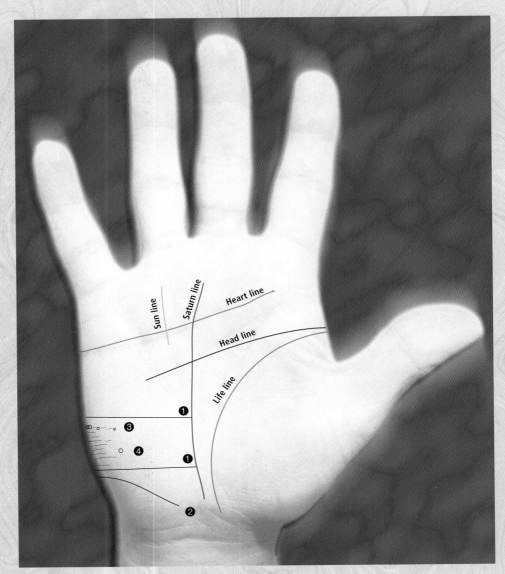

EMIGRATION

When the life line divides into two, one continuing to travel around the Venus mount as usual, while the other runs down on to the base of the Moon mount, it is a strong sign that emigration will be considered. The likelihood can be judged by the respective strength of the two branches of the life line. If the line hugging the Venus mount is more pronounced ❶, the decision will be to stay in the country of origin. Should the line that runs to the Moon mount dominate, the urge to emigrate will win ❷.

On some hands the lines are of equal power, and it is then necessary to look for other clues. If the hand is an adventurous, travel-loving shape – Mars, Moon or Mercury – with a strong head line showing willpower, and a firm thumb, giving resolve, the balance will tip towards emigration. The year of emigration can be judged from the point at which the lifeline divides by referring to that line's dating system.

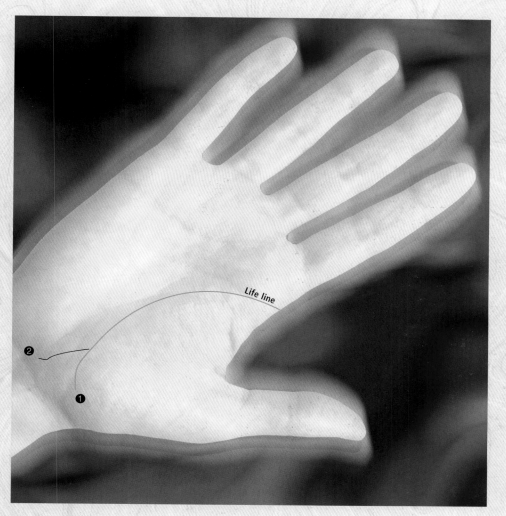

Life line

STARS AND STRIPES

This hand is marked with an array of stars, circles, islands, triangles, squares and grilles. These symbols affect whichever mount, plain or line they appear on, and it is interesting to work out what they mean from the nature of the mount, line or plain.

Squares always preserve from danger, so a square on the Moon mount ❶, which governs the imagination, affords protection from illusions, addictions and overactive, destructive imaginings.

Stars are always fortunate, bringing achievement, respect and renown ❷. A star on a fingertip grants a lucky touch with whatever creativity or careers are associated with that fingertip ❸.

Islands and circles indicate problems and disruptions. If they are on a mount they weaken the personality characteristics linked to that mount. On the Jupiter mount they would suggest low willpower, a lack of ambition and low self-esteem ❹. Grilles have a similar affect but lead to stress and confusion ❺.

Triangles are favourable, emphasizing and boosting the qualities of whichever mount they

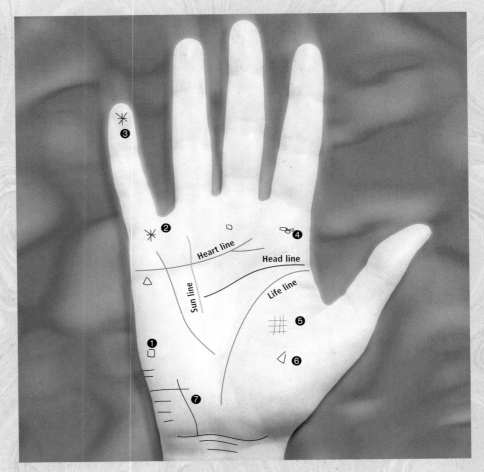

appear on ❻. A triangle on the second Mars mount indicates an excellent sense of strategy, an instinctive understanding of psychology and good reactions in any emergency.

A well-marked travel line leaves the first bracelet and travels to the Moon mount ❼, signifying an important journey, which could be a trip that results in meeting a partner, one that influences the career or one that prompts emigration or a stay abroad.

A CROSS TO BEAR

A cross on the palm is usually a 'cross to bear' – that is, a trouble, problem, disappointment or danger. A cross on the Moon mount ❶, for example, signifies self-deception, addiction, a tendency to live in a fantasy world, a warped imagination and even a period of mental illness.

There is one exception: a cross on the Jupiter mount is a sign of at least one happy marriage or another deeply bonded love relationship ❷. If the cross is low on the Jupiter mount by the life line the union takes place early in life. When the cross is at the mount's centre the match is made in middle age, if it is high up near the base of the Jupiter finger, it is later in life.

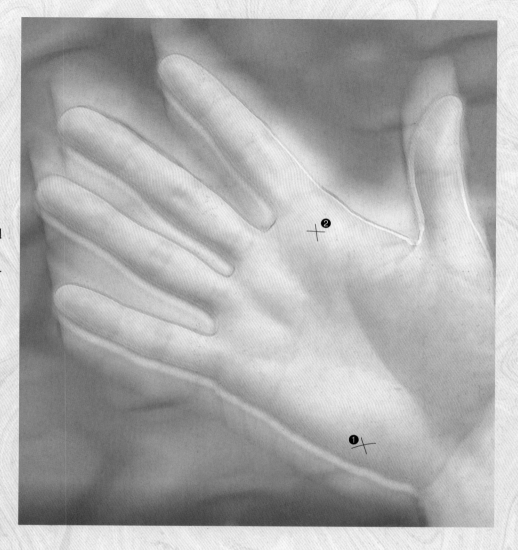

LOOPS AND WHORLS

The two markings illustrated on this hand are skin ridge patterns like fingerprints rather than lines created by movement, such as the head line, life line and so on. The skin ridges move over the whole of the palm and fingers in waves, and their energies are concentrated wherever they eddy into pool-like whorls or loops.

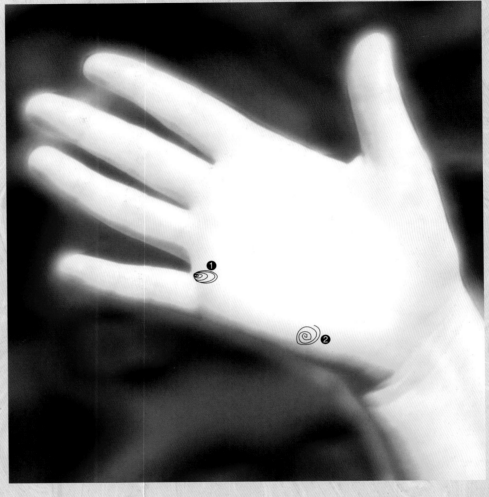

The loop between the Sun finger and the Mercury finger is known as the loop of humour ❶. It grants the gift of being able to make other people laugh. If you have got this pattern on your hand you will possess a robust sense of humour and always appreciate the wit of others. If you are in company you will have the urge to entertain, and will never be afraid to play the fool for laughs.

The whorl on the Moon mount is referred to as the whorl of fantasy ❷. It heightens sensitivity and imagination, so that dreams are vivid. Fantasy worlds will be important to someone with this mark, with fiction and escapist drama being thoroughly enjoyed. Daydreaming will be a talent, and mood swings will be much in evidence, ranging from light-headed and brimming with life to depressed and negative.

This whorl is a sign of creativity and inspiration. The question will be whether these characteristics will be allowed to lie dormant or be used positively.

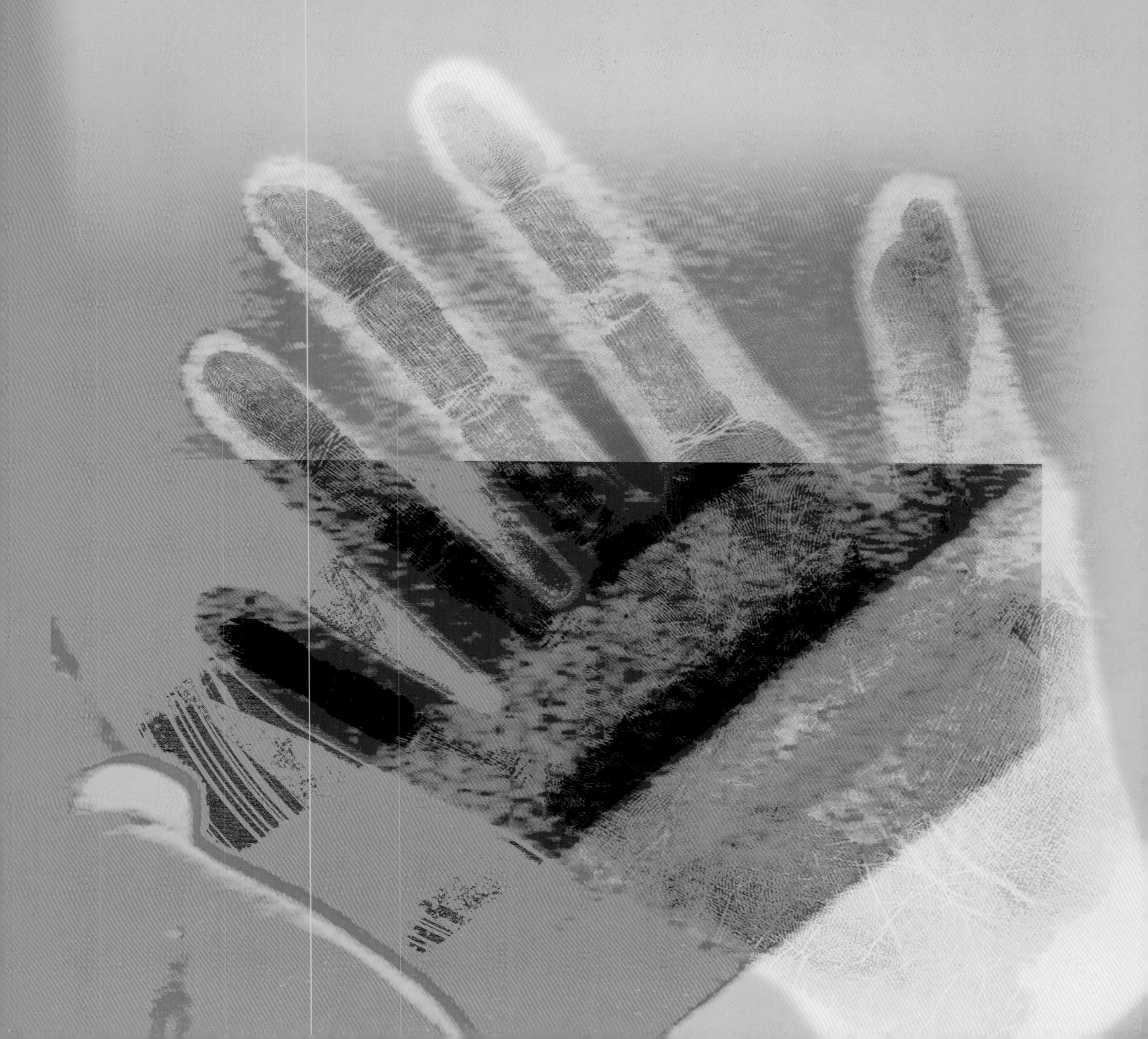

Index

Credits

With grateful thanks to:

Monica Laita from New Division for the artwork on pages:
15, 16, 19, 20, 23, 26, 27, 29, 31, 36, 37, 38, 39, 40, 41, 45, 47,
50, 51, 52, 53, 123, 126, 127, 128, 129, 130.

Caroline Grimshaw who prepared all the other illustrations
of hands.

All those at Chrysalis Books who allowed their hands to be
photographed and reproduced in this book.